CW00550734

CRISES OF DEMOCRACY

Is democracy in crisis? The current threats to democracy are not just
political: they are deeply embedded in the democracies of today, in
current economic, social, and cultural conditions. In *Crises of
Democracy*, Adam Przeworski presents a panorama of the political
situation throughout the world of established democracies, places it
in the context of misadventures of democratic regimes, and
speculates on the prospects. Our present state of knowledge does
not support facile conclusions. We "should not believe the flood of
writings that have all the answers." Avoiding technical aspects, this
book is addressed not only to professional social scientists, but to
everyone concerned about the prospects of democracy.

ADAM PRZEWORSKI is the Carroll and Milton Professor of
Politics and Economics at New York University. A member of the
American Academy of Arts and Sciences since 1991, he is the
recipient of the 1985 Socialist Review Book Award, the 1998
Gregory M. Luebbert Article Award, the 2001 Woodrow Wilson
Prize, the 2010 Lawrence Longley Article Award, the 2018 Sakip
Sabanci International Award, and the 2018 Juan Linz Prize. In 2010,
he received the Johan Skytte Prize. He recently published *Why
Bother with Elections?* (2018).

CRISES OF DEMOCRACY

ADAM PRZEWORSKI
New York University

CAMBRIDGE
UNIVERSITY PRESS

University Printing House, Cambridge CB2 8BS, United Kingdom

One Liberty Plaza, 20th Floor, New York, NY 10006, USA

477 Williamstown Road, Port Melbourne, VIC 3207, Australia

314–321, 3rd Floor, Plot 3, Splendor Forum, Jasola District Centre, New Delhi – 110025, India

79 Anson Road, #06–04/06, Singapore 079906

Cambridge University Press is part of the University of Cambridge.

It furthers the University's mission by disseminating knowledge in the pursuit of education, learning, and research at the highest international levels of excellence.

www.cambridge.org
Information on this title: www.cambridge.org/9781108498807
DOI: 10.1017/9781108671019

First published 2019

Printed in the United Kingdom by TJ International Ltd. Padstow Cornwall

A catalogue record for this publication is available from the British Library.

ISBN 978-1-108-49880-7 Hardback

CONTENTS

CONTENTS

vi

Writing an academic book about current events is perilous. The period between the moment the book is written and the time it is read is long, while political life does not stop in-between. Hence, much information contained below must be read with the caveat "as of such and such date." Yet if a book is worth anything, the arguments and the conclusions should survive the particular events that may have transpired in the meantime. I say this without much confidence: the very event that prompted me to plunge into this volume was something I never expected, the victory of Donald Trump. Yet I think I learned something in retrospect, namely, that the reasons to worry about the current state of democracy in the United States and in some European countries are much deeper than the contingent events. Had Trump lost, many people who are now rushing to write books similar to this one, myself included, would have been occupied by other pursuits. Yet the economic, social, and cultural conditions that brought Trump to office would have been the same. This is what I learned writing this text: that the causes of the current discontent are deep, that they would not have been alleviated by accidental events, and that we need to ask what if Clinton had won or Brexit had lost, and what will happen if and when whatever governments that are now in office in developed democracies fail to improve the lives of people who had voted for them? What then? Where should we seek solutions: in economic policies, in political reforms, in discursive strategies of combating social fragmentation and racism? No answers to such questions are obvious to me, so there is little I try to persuade the readers about. All I can do is to formulate questions, entertain possibilities, and invite the readers to think together.

I present a panorama of the current political situation across the world of well-established democracies, place it in the context of past misadventures of democratic regimes, and speculate about their prospects. I know that some readers will be disappointed by how often I fail to arrive at firm conclusions. But one should not believe the flood of writings that have all the answers. I understand, and share, the quest to find sense in what is happening around us, and the urge to think that the diverse developments that surprise us must be somehow related, that everything must have a cause. Yet establishing what causes what and what matters most is often very difficult and sometimes impossible. Particularly in our perilous times, it is important to know what we do not know before deciding how to act. Hence, I hope to encourage skepticism among those who will read this book only because they are concerned about the prospects of democracy. At the same time, I hope that graduate students and my professional colleagues will find here an agenda for research on questions that are technically difficult and politically important.

The topic of this book concerns the dangers to democracy lurking in the current economic, cultural, and political situation. Yet the greatest danger we face is not to democracy but to humanity, namely, that unless we do something drastic now, immediately, our children will be baked or flooded. If this danger materializes, all our concerns about democracy will become moot. Tragically, this specter receives only scant political attention, and this absence is reflected in the pages that follow. Yet it casts an ominous shadow over everything else we may care about.

Some people have already reacted to various parts of this text, so the current version is indebted to comments by Carlos Acuna, Jose Antonio Aguilar Rivera, Jess Benhabib, Pierre Birnbaum, Bruce Bueno de Mesquita, Zhiyuan Cui, Daniel Cukierman, Larry Diamond, John Dunn, Joan Esteban, Roberto Gargarella, Stephen Holmes, John Ferejohn, Joanne Fox-Przeworski, Fernando Limongi, Zhaotian Luo, Boris Makarenko, Bernard Manin, Jose Maria Maravall, Andrei Melville, Patricio Navia, Gloria Origgi, Pasquale Pasquino, Molly Przeworski, John Roemer, Pacho Sanchez-Cuenca, Aleksander Smolar, Willie Sonnleitner, Milan Svolik, Juan Carlos Torre, Joshua Tucker, Jerzy J. Wiatr, and three anonymous reviewers. I am particularly indebted to John Ferejohn for forcing me to revise the analytical framework.

1

Introduction

> The crisis consists precisely in the fact that the old is dying
> and the new cannot be born; in this interregnum a great
> variety of morbid symptoms appear.
>
> (Antonio Gramsci, *Prison Notebooks*, c.1930: 275–6)

Something is happening. "Anti-establishment," "anti-system," "anti-elite," "populist" sentiments are exploding in many mature democracies. After almost a century during which the same parties dominated democratic politics, new parties are springing up like mushrooms while the support for traditional ones is dwindling. Electoral participation is declining in many countries to historically unprecedented levels. Confidence in politicians, parties, parliaments, and governments is falling. Even the support for democracy as a system of government has weakened. Popular preferences about policies diverge sharply. Moreover, the symptoms are not just political. Loss of confidence in institutions extends to the media, banks, private corporations, even churches. People with different political views, values, and cultures increasingly view each other as enemies. They are willing to do nasty things to each other.

   Is democracy in crisis? Is this change epochal? Are we living through an end of an era? It is easy to become alarmist, so we need to maintain a perspective. Apocalyptic announcements of an "end to" (Western Civilization, History, Democracy) or "death of" (the State, Ideology, Nation-State) are perennial. Such claims are titillating but I cannot think of anything on this list that did end or die. Not yielding to fears, a dose of skepticism, must be the point of departure. The null hypothesis must be that things come and go and there is nothing exceptional about the present moment. After all, it may well be true that, as the Hungarian Marxist Georg Lukács would have it, "crises are but an intensification of everyday life of bourgeois society." Just note that the Harvard Widener library holds more than 23,600 books published in the twentieth century in English containing the word "crisis" (Graf and Jarausch 2017).

Yet many people fear that this time it is different, that at least some established democracies are experiencing conditions that are historically unprecedented, that democracy may gradually deteriorate, "backslide," or even not survive under these conditions.

1.1 Crises of Democracy

What should we be looking for if we fear that democracy is experiencing a crisis? To identify crises of democracy, we need a conceptual apparatus: What is democracy? What is a crisis? Is the crisis already here or is it only impending? If it is already here, how do we recognize it? If it is not yet visible, from what signs do we read the future?

We are repeatedly told that "Unless democracy is X or generates X, ..." The ellipsis is rarely spelled out, but it insinuates either that a particular system is not worthy of being called a "democracy" unless some X is present or that democracy will not endure unless some X is satisfied. The first claim is normative, even if it often hides as a definition. Skinner (1973: 303), for example, thinks that a system in which only some people rule does not merit being called a "democracy," even if it is a competitive oligarchy. Rosanvallon (2009), in turn, claims that "Now power is not considered fully democratic unless it is submitted to the tests of control and validation at the same time concurrent and complementary to the majoritarian expression." The second claim is empirical, namely, that democracy may not endure unless some Xs are present (or absent). If democracy requires some conditions – say J.S. Mill's (1977: 99) "high wages and universal reading" – just to function, then it is vulnerable to breakdowns when these conditions are absent. A modicum of economic welfare, some level of citizen's confidence in political institutions, or some minimal level of public order are the most plausible candidates for such conditions.

Thus, one way to think is that democracy experiences a crisis when some features which we consider as definitional of democracy are absent. Consider a triad of what Ginsburg and Huq (2018a) consider to be "the basic predicates of democracy": competitive elections, liberal rights of speech and association, and the rule of law. If we treat this triad as definitional, we get a ready-made checklist of what we should be looking for to identify crises of democracy: elections that are not competitive, violations of rights, breakdowns of the rule of law. Yet if we believe that democracy may not survive given some particular situation, we may still be worried that it faces a crisis even if no such violations are observed. We may still have a checklist constructed by the definition but now we also have a set of hypotheses that condition the survival of democracy on some potential threats, and we are directed by these hypotheses to examine the particular threats. If such hypotheses are valid, if the survival of democracy depends on some aspects of its performance, and democracy does not generate the required outcomes, a crisis occurs – democracy is in crisis.

Note that some features may be treated alternatively as definitional or as empirical. If one defines democracy as Rosanvallon does, to include contramajoritarian constraints on majority rule, "constitutional democracy," then the erosion of judicial independence is prima facie evidence that something is wrong. But one may also reason that if the judiciary is not independent, the government will be free to do whatever it wants, violate the liberal right, or make elections non-competitive. The problem with adding adjectives to "democracy" is that not all good things must go together. The more features – "electoral," "liberal," "constitutional," "representative," "social" – we add to the definition of democracy, the longer the checklist, and the more crises we will discover. In contrast, the same list can be treated as a set of empirical hypotheses. We can then investigate empirically what are the conditions for elections to be competitive or for rights to be observed or for the rule of law to prevail. If it is true that elections are competitive only if rights are observed and law rules, then taking any one of these features as definitional and treating others as "preconditions" is coextensive. If they are not coextensive, then some kind of definitional minimalism is unavoidable: we must choose one of the potential features as definitional and treat others as hypothetical conditions under which the selected feature is satisfied.

Hence, what we would consider as crises and how we should go about diagnosing them depends on how we think about democracy. The view of democracy I adopt is "minimalist" and "electoralist": democracy is a political arrangement in which people select governments through elections and have a reasonable possibility of removing incumbent governments they do not like (authors who held this view include Schumpeter 1942, Popper 1962, and Bobbio 1987). Democracy is simply a system in which incumbents lose elections and leave when they lose. Hence, I investigate the possible threats to elections becoming non-competitive or inconsequential for whoever remains in power. To repeat, these threats may include violations of the preconditions for contested elections enumerated by Dahl (1971) – the liberal rights and the freedoms – simply because without them the incumbent government could not be defeated. They may also include breakdowns of the rule of law and erosion of the independent power of the judiciary, along with loss of confidence in representative institutions (as in "representative democracy"), acute inequality (as in "social democracy"), or the use of repression to maintain public order ("liberal democracy"). But I treat these violations as potential threats to the ability of citizens to remove governments by elections, not as definitional features of "democracy."

The relation between "democracy" in the minimalist sense and the "rule of law" is particularly complex. First, there are both logical and empirical reasons to question whether supra-majoritarian institutions, such as bicameralism or presidential veto, or counter-majoritarian institutions, such as constitutional courts or independent central banks, are necessary to support the rule of law. Gargarella (2003), for example, lists several mechanisms by which a majority can and would want to constrain itself even in the absence of such institutions. As McGann (2006) observes, there are well-established democracies, including the United Kingdom and Sweden, which have neither a separation of powers nor judicial review of the constitution, and yet in which majorities constrain themselves from violating rights. Indeed, Dixit, Grossman, and Gull (2000: 533) demonstrate logically that violations of rights are likely to be more egregious in the presence of supra-majoritarian institutions once a government enjoys supra-majority support.

Second, I put "rule of law" in quotation marks because, as Sanchez-Cuenca (2003: 62) astutely put it, "The law cannot rule. Ruling is an activity, and laws cannot act." What is typically seen as a relation between democracy and the rule of law is in fact a relation between populated institutions: governments and courts (Ferejohn and Pasquino 2003). Law "rules" when politicians and bureaucrats obey judges, and whether politicians do or do not comply with the instructions of constitutional justices is a contingent outcome of their electoral incentives. Moreover, as will be seen below, it is often next to impossible to determine if some particular measures they adopt do or do not conform to legal or constitutional norms, with individual judgments, including those of constitutional justices, clouded by partisanship. Under democracy, the only effective device for disciplining politicians are elections: as Dixit, Grossman, and Gull (2000: 533) observe, "The ruling individuals must foresee an appreciable chance that their power will come to an end . . . And they must foresee a possibility of regaining power once it is lost." There are two possibilities: (1) politicians (and bureaucrats) obey judges because otherwise they would lose elections, so that "the law" rules; (2) politicians do not obey judges because otherwise they would lose elections – a majority does not want politicians to listen to what the judges tell them they can or cannot do. The rule of law is violated but as long as politicians' actions are motivated by the fear of losing elections, the system is still democratic by the minimalist criterion. Democracy is "illiberal" – a term made fashionable by Zakaria (1997) and embraced by the Hungarian Prime Minister, Viktor Orbán – but it is illiberal because politicians expect that otherwise they would lose elections. Yet, if politicians do not obey the judges even if a majority would want them to because they do not fear elections, the regime is not democratic.

Understood in this way, democracy is a mechanism for processing conflicts. Political institutions manage conflicts in an orderly way by structuring the way social antagonisms are organized politically, absorbing whatever conflicts may threaten public order, and regulating them according to some rules. An institutional order prevails if only those political forces that have institutionally constituted access to the representative system engage in political activities, and if these organizations have incentives to pursue their interests through the institutions and incentives to temporarily tolerate unfavorable outcomes. Specifically, conflicts are orderly if all political forces expect that they may achieve something, at the present or at least in some not too distant future, by processing their interests within the institutional framework while they see little to be gained by actions outside the institutional realm. Hence, democracy works well when whatever the conflicts that arise in society are channeled into and processed through the institutional framework – most importantly elections, but also collective bargaining systems, courts, and public bureaucracies – without preventing anyone from gaining access to these institutions just because of the substance of their demands. To put it succinctly, democracy works when political conflicts are processed in liberty and civil peace.

The conflicts that divide a particular society at a particular time may be more or less intense and may divide the society along different lines depending on whether they concern economic interests, cultural values, symbolic issues, or just fleeting passions. Their forms, their subjects, and their intensity depend on the actions of governments and the alternatives offered by competing political forces. The stakes entailed in institutionalized conflicts do not simply reflect the intensity of antagonisms that arise in a society. Institutional frameworks shape the ways in which social conflicts become politically organized, some increasing and others limiting the stakes in the outcomes of political competition. I argue below (see Chapter 9) that democracy works well when the stakes entailed in institutionalized conflicts are neither too small or too large (for a technical version of this argument, see Przeworski, Rivero, and Xi 2015). The stakes are too low when results of elections have no consequences for people's lives. They are too high when results of elections inflict intolerable costs on the losers. When people believe that results of elections do not make a difference in their lives, they turn against "das System," as in Weimar Germany. When the electoral losers discover that the government pursues policies that significantly hurt their interests or values, they become willing to resist the government by all – including violent – means, as did the bourgeoisie in Chile under President Allende. Hence, democracy works when something is at stake in elections but not too much is at stake.

An often overlooked emphasis of Schumpeter's (1942: chapter 23, section 2) "minimalist" view of democracy is that governments must be able to govern and must govern competently. Later I delve into some historical periods in which the institutional framework made it difficult for governments to be able to govern, either because the electoral system led to government instability, as in Weimar Germany and the French Fourth Republic, or because the system of separation of powers generated a stalemate between the executive and the legislature, as in Allende's Chile. To govern effectively, governments must satisfy a majority yet not ignore the views of intense minorities. When conflicts are intense and a society is highly polarized, finding policies acceptable to all major political forces is difficult and may be impossible. There are limits to what even the best-intentioned and competent governments can do.

If this is the standard, when is democracy "in crisis"? The very word "crisis" originates from ancient Greek, where it meant "decision." Crises are situations that cannot last, in which something must be decided. They emerge when the status quo is untenable and nothing has yet replaced it. This is what we mean when we say that "the situation reached a crisis point": when doctors say someone is in a crisis, they mean that the patient will either recover or die but cannot remain in the current state. Crises may be more or less acute: in some a turning point may be imminent but some crises may linger indefinitely, with all the morbid symptoms.

The intuition of crises conveyed by Gramsci's motto is that the current situation is in some ways untenable, that some threat to democracy has already materialized, yet the status quo democratic institutions remain in place. While Marx (1979 [1859]: 43–4) thought that "new superior relations of production never replace older ones before the material conditions for their existence have matured within the framework of the old society," nothing guarantees that when the status quo institutions malfunction, some other institution would descend on earth as a *deux ex machina*. What happens when the status quo institutions do not generate desirable outcomes depends on their properties and on the alternative institutions – would any do better? – on exogenous conditions, and on the actions of the relevant political forces under these conditions. That a disaster is unfolding under the status quo institutions need not imply that some other institutions would do better: this was Winston Churchill's view of democracy. But even if some alternatives are feasible, it may well be that given the relations of political power under the extant institutions, the situation would linger on and on. Crises are then situations in which the condition under the status quo institutions is some kind of a disaster: no change occurs, but it may. This is what we will be looking for below: whether the current situation is in some ways threatening and whether there are signs that the traditional representative institutions are being affected.

"Crises of capitalism" deserve a separate comment. Capitalism – an institution that combines private ownership of most productive resources with the allocation of resources and distribution of incomes by markets – periodically generates "crises," understood as periods in which incomes fall sharply and either inflation flares or unemployment soars or both, as during the "stagflation crisis" of the 1970s, a combination of high inflation with high unemployment caused by a jump in prices of raw materials (Bruno and Sachs 1985). But are economic crises "crises of capitalism"? They would be if one expects that when the economy is in the doldrums, capitalism will or at least may collapse. But an implosion of capitalism is not in the realm of the possible. When a famous leftist economist, Michal Kalecki (1972 [1932]), asked in 1932, at the worst moment of the Great Depression, "Is a capitalist exit from the crisis possible?," his argument was that, even if the adjustments required to exit from economic crises are painful and may take time, capitalism is a self-correcting system. Prices and wages may be sticky but eventually supply and demand adjust, the crisis is over, and capitalism is still here. It can be abolished by a political revolution – a possibility Kalecki did entertain and Communists implemented – but not implode. The general lesson for understanding crises is that some institutions are impervious to the outcomes they generate, so that crises which occur under them do not turn into crises of the institutions.

Disasters that occur under democracy, however, may turn into crises of democracy. Borrowing their list from Habermas (1973: 49), disasters are situations in which

- the economic system does not produce the requisite quantity of consumable values, or;
- the administrative system does not produce the requisite quantity of rational decisions, or;
- the legitimation system does not provide the requisite quantity of generalized motivations, or;
- the socio-cultural system does not generate the requisite quantity of action-motivating meaning.

This list, however, is too abstract to guide research. The observable candidates for disasters are economic crises, intense conflicts in society, and political paralyses, situations in which the government is unable to govern given the particular form of democratic institutions.

When we think that the situation is in some way threatening, we look for signals – harbingers of change. Several countries, ranging from Canada in 1931–3 to Uruguay in 2001–3, experienced profound economic crises with almost no political repercussions and no signals of democracy being weakened. Yet in some situations crises in other realms – whether economic, cultural, or autonomously political (say corruption scandals, as in Italy in 1993 or in Brazil now) – manifestly weaken the established democratic institutions. The visible signals that democracy is in crisis include a sudden loss of support for established parties, withdrawal of popular confidence in democratic institutions and politicians, overt conflicts over democratic institutions, or an incapacity of governments to maintain public order without repression. Perhaps the most tangible sign of a crisis is a breakdown of public order: in the words of Linz (1978: 54), "The most serious crises are those in which the maintenance of public order becomes impossible within a democratic framework." Democracy is in crisis when fists, stones, or bullets replace ballots. Either the incumbents make it impossible for the opposition to remove them from office and the opposition has no other avenues than resistance, or the opposition does not recognize the legitimacy of the government and the government defends itself by repression, or antagonistic political groups do not accept the outcomes of the institutional interplay of interests and revert to direct, often violent, confrontations. When such situations extend over time, public order breaks down, everyday life becomes paralyzed, and violence tends to spiral. Such crises become mortal when the design of democratic institutions generates institutional stalemates, as in Weimar Germany or in Chile under President Allende.

Institutions may generate outcomes that are intolerable for some and wonderful for others. Moreover, people may differ in their normative attachments: some valuing liberty more than order, others being willing to sacrifice it for the promise that trains would run on time (Mussolini promised they would under fascism, but they did not). Hence, to understand crises it is necessary to think in terms of conflicting interests and values. The poor are dissatisfied when their incomes stagnate, the rich enjoy their wealth and power, while some people, whether poor or wealthy, may care about political and economic inequality per se. Solutions to crises are likely to be controversial and subject to political conflicts. They depend on what the relevant political actors do under the circumstances. To this extent, therefore, they are indeterminate *ex ante*. Will a reduction of economic inequalities restore the political vitality of democracy? Will restrictions on immigration appease radical Right sentiments? Will some tinkering with representative institutions restore confidence in these institutions? Because the actors in crisis may choose different courses of actions, with different consequences, the best we can strive to determine is what is and what is not possible, perhaps with some cavalier forecasts about what is most likely.

What, then, are the possible outcomes of crises? Not all crises are mortal: some end in restoring the status quo ante, a return to "normalcy." The sources of a crisis sometimes conveniently disappear. Democracy may be in a crisis when society experiences an economic disaster, but the crisis may dissipate when prosperity returns. Some crises can be overcome by partial reforms. The group that benefits under extant institutions can make concessions to the groups that suffer most under them. Such concessions have to be credible, because otherwise these groups will expect that they would be withdrawn once the crisis is over. Hence, concessions must entail some institutional reforms: the classical example is the extension of suffrage to the lower classes, which neutralized the threat of revolution by changing the income location of the decisive voter (Acemoglu and Robinson 2000). Yet when we think about democracy what we fear is the prospect that some political forces would successfully claim that the only way to remedy some already occurring disasters – economic crises, deep-rooted divisions in society, breakdown of public order – is to abandon political liberty, unite under a strong leader, and repress pluralism of opinions, in short autocracy, authoritarianism, or dictatorship, whatever one wants to call it. The impending cataclysm is that democracy would either collapse outright or gradually erode beyond the point of no return.

The specter that haunts us today, I believe, is the last possibility: a gradual, almost imperceptible, erosion of democratic institutions and norms, subversion of democracy by stealth, "the use of legal mechanisms that exist in regimes with favorable democratic credentials for anti-democratic ends" (Varol 2015). Without manifest signs that democracy has broken down, the line becomes thin, as evidenced by labels such as "electoral authoritarianism" (Schedler 2006), "competitive authoritarianism" (Levitsky and Way 2010), "illiberal democracy" (Zakaria 1997), or "hybrid regimes" (Karl 1995, Diamond 2002). "Backsliding," "deconsolidation," or "retrogression" need not entail violations of constitutionality and yet gradually destroy democratic institutions.

To summarize this concept of "crisis of democracy," think schematically as follows. Given some exogenous shocks, democracy generates some outcomes, positively or negatively evaluated by people with heterogeneous preferences over these outcomes and over the democratic institutions per se. Outcomes that threaten the continued existence of the traditional democratic institutions constitute "disasters." Whether a particular situation qualifies as a crisis must be read from some manifest signals that democratic institutions are under threat. We are attentive to such signals because they may constitute harbingers of democratic collapse or gradual erosion. Yet the potential solutions to crises may include restoration of the institutional status quo, some partial reforms of traditional representative institutions that still preserve democracy, as well as its either abrupt or gradual destruction.

Why would democracies be vulnerable to crises? One must not forget that democracy is but a speck of human history, recent and still rare. It was born only in 1788, when the first national-level election based on individual suffrage took place in the United States; the first time in history that the helm of the government changed as a result of an election was in 1801, also in the United States. Use of force – coups and civil wars – remained frequent: between 1788 and 2008 political power changed hands as a result of 544 elections and 577 coups. Electoral defeats of those in power were rare until very recently and peaceful changes of governments even less frequent: only about one in five national elections resulted in the defeat of incumbents and even fewer in a peaceful change in office. As of today, sixty-eight countries, including the two behemoths, China and Russia, have never experienced a change in office between parties as a result of an election. Democracy is a historical phenomenon. It developed under specific conditions. It survived in some countries as these conditions evolved, but can it survive under all conditions?

Two structural conditions, I think, deserve special attention. The first is that political equality, which democracy is supposed to be based on, coexists uneasily with capitalism, a system of economic inequality. The second is the sheer quest for political power, whether or not based on economic interests.

1.2 Democracy and Capitalism

The relation between democracy and capitalism is subject to contrasting views. One claims a natural affinity of "economic freedom" and "political freedom." Economic freedom means that people can decide what to do with their property and their labor endowments. Political freedom means that they can publicize their opinions and participate in choosing how and by whom they will be governed. But equating the concepts of "freedom" in the two realms is just a play on words. Looking into history shows that we should be surprised by the coexistence of capitalism and democracy. In societies in which only some people enjoy productive property and in which incomes are unequally distributed by markets, political equality combined with majority rule presents a threat to property. Indeed, beginning with Henry Ireton's speech in the franchise debate at Putney in 1647, almost everyone had thought that they could not coexist. The English conservative historian and politician Thomas Macaulay (1900: 263) vividly summarized in 1842 the danger presented to property by universal suffrage:

> The essence of the Charter is universal suffrage. If you withhold that, it matters not very much what else you grant. If you grant that, it matters not at all what else you withhold. If you grant that, the country is lost ... My firm conviction is that, in our country, universal suffrage is incompatible, not only with this or that form of government, and with everything for the sake of which government exists; that it is incompatible with property and that it is consequently incompatible with civilization.

Nine years later, from the other extreme of the political spectrum, Karl Marx (1952: 62) expressed the same conviction that private property and universal suffrage are incompatible:

> The classes whose social slavery the constitution is to perpetuate, proletariat, peasantry, petty bourgeoisie, it [the constitution] puts in possession of political power through universal suffrage. And from the class whose old social power it sanctions, the bourgeoisie, it withdraws the political guarantees of this power. It forces the political rule of the bourgeoisie into democratic conditions, which at every moment jeopardize the very foundations of bourgeois society. From the ones it demands that they should not go forward from political to social emancipation; from the others they should not go back from social to political restoration.

The combination of democracy and capitalism was thus for Marx an inherently unstable form of organization of society, "only the political form of revolution of bourgeois society and not its conservative form of life" (1934 [1852]: 18), "only a spasmodic, exceptional state of things ... impossible as the normal form of society" (1971 [1872]: 198).

These dire predictions turned out to be false. In some – specifically thirteen countries – democracy and capitalism coexisted without interruptions for at least a century, and in many other countries for shorter but nevertheless extended periods, most of which continue today. Working-class parties that had hoped to abolish the private property of productive resources realized that this goal is unfeasible, and learned to value democracy and to administer capitalist economies whenever elections brought them into office. Trade unions, also originally viewed as a mortal threat to capitalism, learned to moderate their demands. The outcome was a compromise: working-class parties and trade unions consented to capitalism, while bourgeois political parties and organizations of employers accepted some redistribution of income. Governments learned to organize this compromise: regulate working conditions, develop social insurance programs, and equalize opportunities, while promoting investment and counteracting economic cycles (Przeworski 1986).

Yet perhaps this compromise is now broken. Unions lost much of their capacity to organize and discipline workers and with it their monopoly power. Socialist parties lost their class roots and with them their ideological as well as policy distinctiveness. The most visible effect of these changes is the sharp decline in the share of incomes from employment in the value added and, at least in the Anglo-Saxon countries, a steep increase of income inequality. Combined with a slowdown of growth, rising inequality causes many incomes to stagnate and income mobility to decline.

Is the coexistence of democracy and capitalism conditional on a continual improvement of material conditions of broad sectors of the population, either because of growth or because of increasing equality? History indicates that democracies are solidly entrenched in economically developed countries and impervious to economic as well as other crises, even of a large magnitude. But is history a reliable guide to the future?

1.3 Democracy and the Quest for Power

The second reason democracies may experience crises is inherent in political competition. The dream of all politicians is to conquer power and to hold on to it forever. It is unreasonable to expect that competing parties would abstain from doing whatever they can do to enhance their electoral advantage, and incumbents have all kinds of instruments to defend themselves from the voice of the people. They are able to consolidate their advantage because they constitute a legislative majority and because they direct public bureaucracies. Although at times they are constrained by independent courts, control over legislation grants incumbents an opportunity to adopt legal regulation in their favor: just think of voter registration, manipulation of electoral systems, or gerrymandering. The courts or some other independent bodies may invalidate some such attempts but not always have reasons or the will to do so: there are many ways to carve districts, each with electoral consequences, which are not blatantly discriminatory. In turn, as principals of ostensibly non-partisan bureaucracies, incumbents can instrumentalize them for partisan purposes. Control over the apparatuses of repression plays a particularly important role in undermining all or some opposition. Exchange of favors for financial resources is yet another source of advantage. And, when all else fails, fraud is the last resort.

The question is why some political leaders use these methods while others are content with letting the people decide and being willing to leave office when people do so decide. Their motives matter and so do the constraints. When political parties are highly ideological, when they believe that essential issues or values are at stake, they see their opponents as enemies who must be prevented from coming to office by any means. In Poland the ruling party, PiS (Law and Justice), believes that the very values that constitute Poland as a Christian Nation are at stake and all their opponents are "traitors." In Hungary, President Orbán thinks that what is at stake is whether "Europe will remain the continent for Europeans." Hence, both attempt to control the media, restrict freedom of association, pack state agencies with their partisan supporters, and toy with electoral rules. These actions are intended to relax the electoral constraints they face, and to make an electoral victory of the opposition next to impossible. Yet they still face political, rather than narrowly electoral, constraint: various forms of popular resistance, such as mass demonstrations, political strikes, or riots. They face the danger that political conflicts could spill out of institutional bounds, resulting in a breakdown of public order. They may or may not take this risk, and if they do, democracy is in crisis.

1.4 A Preview

How then should we go about determining if democracy is presently in crisis, or at least if a crisis is impending?

To look into the future, to identify the possibilities latent in the current situation, we first need to see if we can learn something from the past. Under what conditions did democratic institutions fail to absorb and peacefully regulate conflicts? To answer this question, Part I summarizes the historical experience of all democracies that have been at one time or another consolidated, in the sense of having experienced at least two peaceful alternations in office that resulted from elections, comparing some observable conditions of the democracies that fell and those that survived. Such comparisons, however, are inevitably static, while the outcomes that emerge under any conditions are highly contingent, depending on who does what when. To develop intuitions, I delve in more detail into four cases: the Weimar Republic between 1928 and 1933, and Chile between 1970 and 1973, are two flagrant instances in which democracy succumbed, while France and the United States in the 1960s are cases of political repression and breakdown of order that were resolved institutionally.

Yet history does not speak for itself. Can we trust its lessons? Lessons from history are relatively reliable when current conditions imitate those observed in some past, but iffy when they are unprecedented (King and Zheng 2007). Hence, to see if history can be our guide, we need to compare the current situation with those of the past. Do the current conditions resemble those of democracies that fell or of those that survived? Or are they unprecedented? Some aspects of the current situation are new, in particular a rapid destabilization of traditional party systems. So is the stagnation of low incomes as well as the erosion of the belief in material progress. But causal links are far from obvious. Is the current political conjuncture driven by economic trends or by cultural transformations, or is it autonomous from changes in the economy and society? At what level should we seek explanations: general trends, such as globalization, or specific situations of particular individuals, say those who fear losing decently paying jobs? These are the questions considered in Part II.

To assess the prospects for the future, we need to understand how democracy works when it works well, which is the subject of the theoretical chapter that opens Part III. With this understanding, we can consider the foreboding and uncharted possibility of a gradual erosion of democracy, its subversion by elected governments. Finally, even if we cannot tell what is most likely to ensue, we can at least speculate about what is and what is not possible. Can it happen here?

Part I

The Past: Crises of Democracy

To see what we can learn from history, we need to examine the experience of democracies that had during some periods functioned according to institutional rules. These are democracies in which control over governments changed as a result of elections at least twice without their result being resisted by force. The reason for limiting the cases in this way is that we need to examine democracies in which competing parties had learned that losing elections is not a disaster, that one can lose and come back to office again, and in which the political forces behind the electoral parties had a chance to see that they could protect or advance their interests by directing their efforts within the institutional framework. The number of such democracies is quite large: since 1918, there were eighty-eight democracies that satisfy the criterion of having had at least two alternations in office.

Thirteen of these democracies collapsed in a palpable way. Note, however, that the line dividing democracies from non-democracies, or whatever one wants to call them, is not always clear. Even thirty years ago, when Alvarez et al. (1996) tried to classify regimes as democracies and dictatorships, there was a class of cases about which it was impossible to tell. They were epitomized by Botswana, a country in which all the liberal freedoms seemed to be respected but the same party always won elections, for thirty years and by now for almost sixty. The solution to this difficulty that subsequently became fashionable was to use a trichotomous classification, introducing "hybrid regimes," "semi-authoritarianism," or "electoral authoritarianism," but these labels just cover up the fact that there are situations which we do not know how to classify. Now, as regimes that allow some opposition but still assure themselves of winning elections proliferate rapidly, the problem has become much worse. The central point of Chapter 10 is that when democracies "backslide" there is no clear line to cross. I look at classifications of Venezuela in several data sources, only to learn that no one agrees whether it is still a democracy and if not as of when. So in the end there are some cases in which the collapse of democracy is manifest, marked by some discrete event, but there are some in which democracy slides down a continuous slope, so not only do we not have discrete markers but we can reasonably disagree about whether a particular regime is still democratic or already past the point of no return. I consider here only those breakdowns of democracy that have been marked by some discrete, manifest events, and discuss gradual erosion of democracy in Chapter 10.

Following Magaloni (2017), among the manifest deaths of democracy we should still distinguish different ways in which democracies fall: some are destroyed by military coups while others die when politicians who accede to office in a legal way succeed in removing all institutional checks on their power and in eradicating all organized opposition. Coups – at least those that lead to a death of democracy, such as in Chile in 1973 – are conspicuous events. Usurpations of power by incumbents may be slow and gradual, but in many cases the breakpoints are obvious. The legal end of the Weimar democracy was signaled by a discrete event: the authorization by the Reichstag (the parliament) on March 23, 1933 for the government to act in non-constitutional ways. In Estonia, the breakdown of democracy was marked by the declaration of martial law and the postponement of elections by the prime minister, Konstantin Pats, on March 12, 1934.

To see if history can direct us to what we should be paying attention to in analyzing the current situation, I compare some observable conditions of the democracies that survived and fell in the past. I focus in particular on the effects of different kinds of crises: economic, cultural, or political. These comparisons, however, tell us little about the contingent dynamics of crises, the denouement of events under the various conditions. Hence, I delve into some prominent crises under which democracy fell or survived. Finally, I search for lessons, asking what we should look for in the current political situation if the past were to repeat itself.

2

General Patterns

The aim of this chapter is to examine whether the collapses and survival of democracy are associated with some observable differences between countries that experienced such outcomes. Obviously I am not the first to do so: the literature on the topic is voluminous and by now technically sophisticated. Almost everyone agrees that democracies are unlikely to collapse in economically developed countries; there is strong evidence that in less developed countries democracies are vulnerable to income inequality, and that the longer they have been around the more likely they are to still exist. Whether anything else matters – institutional frameworks, ethno-linguistic or religious fractionalization, educational levels, etc. (the list is long) – is more controversial. While limiting the scope to democracies that at some time became consolidated, the analysis here reproduces some of these findings. My particular interest is in the effect of different kinds of crises: economic, broadly political, and narrowly governmental. The statistical analyses presented below are purely descriptive, so no inferences about causality should be drawn. The role of this chapter in the context of the book is only to arrive at a list of factors that may inform us regarding what to look for in the present situation.

The consolidated democracies that collapsed are listed in Table 2.1. Those that are still around include four African countries (Benin, Cape Verde, Ghana, and

Table 2.1 *Democracies which experienced at least two alternations after 1918 and subsequently fell*

Country	Year second	Year fell	Alternations	Mode
Germany	1928	1933	3	From above
Estonia	1932	1934	2	From above
Greece	1951	1967	2	Coup
Chile	1952	1973	4	Coup
Sri Lanka	1960	1977	3	From above
Philippines	1961	1965	2	From above
Solomon Islands	1989	2000	2	Coup
Peru	1990	1990	2	Legal
Ecuador	1992	2000	3	Coup
Thailand	1996	2006	3	Coup
Pakistan	1997	1999	2	Coup
Bangladesh	2001	2007	2	From above
Honduras	2005	2009	2	Coup

Note: In order of dates of the second alternation. "Alternations" is the number of alternations by the time democracy fell. Mode: "From above" if power was usurped by a chief executive who came into office in a constitutional way, "Coup" if democracy fell because of a military coup. Only the breakdowns marked by discrete events are included. Source: Boix, Miller, and Rosato (2012) for regime classification, own research for the mode.

Mauritius), eleven Central and South American countries, several Caribbean and small Pacific islands, India, Indonesia, Taiwan, and all the current members of the OECD.

The remaining democracies survived, but it does not mean that they did not face some kind of disaster. Several countries where democracy survived experienced serious economic crises – which I take as periods in which per capita incomes fell by at least 10 percent during

Table 2.2 *Incidence of economic crises and survival of democracy*

Crises	Survived	Fell	Total	Incidence
None	66	10	76	1/7.6
Yes	9	3	12	1/4.0
Total	75	13	88	1/6.8

Note: Crises are situations in which per capita income fell by at least 10 percent during consecutive years. Cell entries are numbers of countries. Sources: Maddison (2011) for income data, Boix, Miller, and Rosato (2012) for regime classification.

consecutive years – without major political repercussions: Canada (1931–3), the United States (1932–4 and 1946–8), the United Kingdom (1946–7), Jamaica (1976–8), Costa Rica (1982–3), Finland (1992–3), Venezuela (1980–5), and Uruguay (2001–3). Indeed, only three consolidated democracies fell following thus-defined economic crises: Germany in 1933, Ecuador in 2000, and Peru in 1990. Hence, transformations of economic into political crises are far from automatic. Lindvall (2014) compared the electoral effects of the economic crises of 1929–32 and 2008–11, finding that they were very similar. In both periods incumbents lost votes, and in both periods elections that occurred soon after the crisis favored the Right, while those that occurred later generated no swing or a swing to the Left. Hence, if a democracy survives an economic crisis, its electoral effects are short-lived.

Several democracies overcame political crises. In Table 2.2, I count as political crises situations: in which there are conflicting claims as to who should govern; where the competent courts declare the government to have violated the constitution or its members to be legally unfit to continue serving (typically accused of corruption); when a conflict between separate powers renders the government unable to function; or where a government is forced to resign or repress the opposition either because of popular pressures or a threat from the military, rather than by a decision of the competent body (either the legislature or the courts). Extended negotiations over government formation in parliamentary systems – the record holder as of now is Belgium, where negotiations took 353 days in 2011 – are not considered as crises, and neither are impeachment procedures in presidential systems if succession follows constitutional rules in a timely manner. Such crises occurred in ten consolidated democracies that did survive. In chronological order, they erupted in France in 1958, the United States in 1973–4, Jamaica in 1983, the Dominican Republic in 1994, Guyana in 1997, Argentina in 2001–3, Romania in 2007, Ukraine in 2014, Mauritius in 2014, and Guatemala in 2014–15. Most of these crises were terminated by a subsequent election. Notably, the institutional status quo ante was restored in all cases except for France, where the crisis resulted in a change of the constitution. Yet, as Table 2.3 shows, such political crises are dangerous: five out of fifteen democracies that experienced them collapsed.

What, then, are the differences between those democracies that fell and those that continue to function, including those that experienced political and economic crises? Unfortunately, systematic information is scarce. But some patterns stand out.

Table 2.3 *Incidence of political crises and survival of democracy*

Crises	Survived	Fell	Total	Incidence
None	65	8	73	1/9.1
Yes	10	5	15	1/3.0
Total	75	13	88	1/6.8

Note: Crises as defined in the body of the text. Cell entries are numbers of countries. Sources: Own research for crises, Boix, Miller, and Rosato (2012) for regime classification.

The most striking difference, which will not surprise students of regime transitions, is in per capita income. We have known for some time that democracies are impregnable in economically developed countries. Przeworski and Limongi (1997) observed that the probability of democracy surviving increases steeply as income increases, and that no democracy in a country with per capita income higher than that of Argentina in 1976 has ever collapsed, although it did collapse in Thailand in 2006 with income slightly higher. The general pattern, however, remains the same and, as Table 2.4 shows, it holds strongly for the consolidated democracies as well. Sixty-nine consolidated democracies lasted a total of 1957 years with incomes higher than that of Thailand in 2006 and none of them fell.

Economic growth was much slower in democracies that fell than in those that survived. The difference is big: economies of countries where democracy fell were almost completely stagnant. Using a different source, Maddison (2011), which includes

Table 2.4 *Some differences between democracies that fell and did not before 2008*

	Survived	Survived	Fell	Fell	Probability[e]
	N	Mean	N	Mean	
GDP/cap[a]	1,484	18,012	103	5,770	1.00
Growth[a]	1,471	0.031	103	0.011	1.00
Labor share[a]	1,397	0.60	96	0.50	1.00
Gini gross[b]	1,148	42.6	64	44.6	1.00
Gini net[b]	1,148	33.8	64	44.6	1.00
Regime[c]	1,739	0.55	124	1.18	1.00
Government crises[d]	1,689	0.17	140	0.44	1.00
Riots[d]	1,689	0.53	140	0.73	0.89
Strikes[d]	1,689	0.13	140	0.26	0.99
Demonstrations[d]	1,689	0.64	140	0.63	0.49

Note: Cell entries are numbers of annual observations (until 2014) and the average values of the particular variables. (a) From PWT9.0. (b) Gini coefficients of gross and net incomes, from SWIID (2014). (c) Regime = 0 if parliamentary, Regime = 1 if mixed, Regime = 2 if presidential, from Cheibub, Gandhi, and Vreeland (2010). (d) From CNTSDA, Wilson (2017). (e) The probability that the difference of the means is not a matter of chance. Based on t-test with unequal variances.

an earlier period and ends in 2008, shows an even larger difference. Hence, even if short-term economic crises do not threaten democracy, protracted stagnation of incomes may.

While the number of observations is low, it is also clear that democracies that fell had a more unequal distribution of income. In functional terms, labor share was lower in democracies that fell. The Gini index of gross (market, pre-fisc) incomes was higher among democracies that fell, as was the inequality of net (post-fisc) incomes. The comparison of these indices indicates that democracies that survived were those which redistributed a fair part of incomes, while those that fell redistributed none.

Moving beyond the economy, another striking difference is among the democratic systems of institutions: parliamentary, mixed (semi-presidential), and presidential. The weakness of presidential democracies is manifest. There were forty-four consolidated parliamentary democracies and of those six fell, 1 in 7.3; sixteen mixed (or semi-presidential) systems of which one fell, and twenty-six presidential ones of which six fell, 1 in 3.7. This difference need not be due to these systems per se: Cheibub (2007: chapter 6) shows that presidential democracies are brittle when they succeed military, but not civilian, dictatorships. Yet, given the traditional role of the military in Latin America, presidential democracies were particularly vulnerable to crises of governance. The major difference between parliamentary and presidential systems is that the former have a built-in mechanism for changing governments that cannot cope with crises and become unpopular: the vote of non-confidence in the government. In presidential systems, however, the chief executive is elected for a fixed term and appoints his or her cabinet, at most subject to congressional approval. Unless the president commits illegal acts, he remains in office regardless of his capacity to govern, even when his popularity reaches single-digit numbers and he has no support in the legislature.

The frequency of government crises is also sharply higher in those democracies that fell. This information has to be taken with a grain of salt: its source, the Cross-National Time-Series Data Archive (CNTSDA) (Wilson 2017) provides

Table 2.5 *Probability of democratic breakdown, given the number of governmental crises and institutional systems*

Crises[a]	Parliamentary	Presidential	Total
0	0.030 (1,213)	0.097 (496)	0.048 (2,184)
1	0.045 (157)	0.320 (37)	0.087 (242)
2	0.120 (33)	0.333 (9)	0.158 (57)
> 2	0.00 (7)	0.430 (7)	0.221 (23)
Total	0.034 (1,410)	0.120 (549)	0.057 (2478)
Probabilities[b]	0.115	0.000	0.000
Gamma	0.154	0.092	0.081

Note: Cell entries are the probabilities that democracy would fall given the number of crises, with numbers of observations in parentheses. (a) Number of crises during a particular year. (b) The probabilities are that the value of the statistic below is higher than a threshold value (statistical significance of the differences). Sources: Own research for crises, Cheibub, Gandhi, and Vreeland (2010) for the institutional systems, Boix, Miller, and Rosato (2012) for regime classification.

only a vague definition of "major government crises" and warns that the data may not be reliable. Nevertheless, comparing the proportions of democracies that fell under different institutional arrangements given government crises shows that presidential systems are highly vulnerable once a government crisis explodes. Table 2.5 shows that the effects of such crises are not statistically significant in parliamentary systems, but they are in systems that have directly elected presidents.

A puzzling feature of the patterns shown in Table 2.4 is the difference among different forms of popular mobilization against the government. Again, one should not put too much credence in the data, but it is startling that while those democracies that fell had higher frequencies of general strikes and riots, the frequency of anti-government demonstrations was the same. It bears emphasis that the mere appearance of masses of people on the streets need not indicate a crisis. In some democracies, peaceful demonstrations are a standard repertoire of democratic politics, a routine way to inform the government that some people feel intensely about some issues, whether in support of or in opposition to government policies. The propensity to hit the streets differs greatly across democracies – it is frequent in France and extremely rare in Norway, frequent in Argentina and rare in Costa Rica, reflecting perhaps differences in political culture. What the statistical patterns seem to indicate is that recourse to anti-government demonstrations is just an aspect of everyday life in democracies. A caveat is obvious, however, and will appear prominently below: as long as these demonstrations do not lead to physical violence.

Finally, a crucial factor not considered thus far is the past experience of democracy. Cornell, Møller, and Skaaning (2017) warn against drawing analogies between the collapse of democracies in the interwar years and the present situation. Notably, they show that in spite of the turbulence of the interwar period, none of the twelve democracies that existed for at least ten years before World War I fell, while twelve of the fifteen democracies that were born right before or after the war collapsed during the interwar period. More generally, Przeworski (2015) learned that the probability of a democracy falling decreases rapidly as a country accumulates the experience of peaceful alternations in office resulting from elections. Among the eighty-eight consolidated democracies, one in ten collapsed when the particular democratic spell witnessed no more than three alternations and only one, in Chile, fell when the number of past alternations reached four.[1]

Putting these patterns together, here are the lessons one can draw from these comparisons of democracies that fell with those that survived. The economy matters: both the income at which democracies are consolidated and subsequent economic growth sharply distinguish the different outcomes. Inequality, functional and household, also matters. Presidential democracies are more likely to fall, being particularly vulnerable to governmental crises. Finally, while riots and strikes weaken democracy, as long as they are not violent we should not fear that anti-government demonstrations would undermine it.

---

[1] Below I use a count of "unrest" several times: the sum of riots, assassinations, general strikes, and anti-government demonstrations, from a data collection originated by Banks (1996) and continued by Wilson (2017), which I refer to as CNTSDA. These data seem comparable across countries and time during the early period, but appear to suffer a bias resulting from increased media coverage during the recent period and from unequal attention to small and large countries.

3

Some Stories

The comparisons presented above are static: they just summarize average conditions of democracies that survived with those that collapsed. But histories unravel as sequences of contingent events, and are not uniquely determined by the extant conditions. Not all that did happen had to happen. To capture these contingent dynamics, I relate four stories: the collapses of democracy in Weimar Germany and in Chile and the institutionally resolved political crises in the United States and in France. I include Germany – a case in which a politician came to office constitutionally and usurped power, still constitutionally, while already in office – because the collapse of the Weimar democracy is widely used as an omen. I include Chile because *mutatis mutandis* it was a paradigmatic case in which the military acted in defense of capitalism, and democracy fell via a military coup. The political crises in the United States and France shared the combination of intense conflicts over foreign wars with highly divisive domestic issues. In the United States under Nixon the danger was the usurpation of power by the incumbent, while in France at the end of the 1950s the threat was a military coup, so these cases parallel those of, respectively, Germany and Chile. In both countries the crises were institutionally resolved but in contrasting ways: in the United States the extant institutions overcame the crisis and remained intact, while in France the solution involved conflict and entailed major institutional reforms.

39

In each case I first briefly describe the past history of a particular spell of democracy and then follow the schematic analysis of crises announced above. I identify the "disaster(s)" that exposed democracy to a threat, I look for the signs that democracy was being weakened, and finally I describe the outcomes of the crises. Because each of these histories is a subject of many existing volumes, the few pages dedicated to them below must abstract from many complexities. Moreover, these were dramatic situations that evoked political passions not only at the time, but that continue to evoke controversies, some still intensely partisan, until today. My only purpose in recounting them is to search for lessons that may illuminate our current political situation, so their presentation is inevitably partial and schematic. What I want to understand is how the crises emerged and how they were resolved, by force or by recourse to institutions.

3.1 Germany, 1928–1933

1. Democracy. Democracy, or more accurately "Republic," was an improvised solution to the external pressure to abolish the monarchy, from the onset seen by several political forces as a temporary one. It did enjoy the support of voters: the "Weimar Coalition" of the Social Democratic Party (SPD), the Catholic Zentrum Party (Z), and the German Democratic Party (DDP) received 76 percent of the vote in the election of 1919. But several sectors of the Right were either monarchist or authoritarian and never accepted the republican form of government, while the extreme Left, first the Independent Social Democratic Party (USPD) and then the Communist

Party (KPD) was committed to a socialist revolution, if need be by force.

Nevertheless, until 1930 German governments were formed as the result of elections. The first alternation occurred in 1920, when the SPD was forced to leave the government led by a Zentrum Prime Minister (PM), Konstantin Fehrenbach, and the second in 1928, when the SPD returned to the government with Hermann Muller becoming the PM (even if the Zentrum remained in the government coalition).

2. Threats. The Weimar Republic was born out of the disaster of Germany's defeat in World War I. During the entire life of the Weimar Republic the terms of the settlement of the war – the conditions of the Armistice of November 1918 and of the Versailles Treaty of 1919 (the abandonment of a monarchical form of government, the loss of territory, the prohibition of unification with Austria, the prohibition on rearmament, and the reparations) – continued to be extremely divisive.

Economic disasters struck twice. Income inequality was not particularly high: according to Jung (2011: 31), the Gini coefficient was about 0.33, while inferring it from the data on top incomes (Atkinson, Piketty, and Saenz 2011) yields a Gini of about 0.36. Yet the history of Weimar was punctuated by two economic crises: the hyperinflation of 1923 and the unemployment resulting from the crash of 1929. The hyperinflation redistributed incomes from savers to borrowers, with average income falling by 17.4 percent. The unemployment rate rose from about 3 percent in 1925 to 12 percent in mid-1930 and to 25 percent by 1932, with civilian employment falling from about 20 million in 1928 to about 13 million in the first quarter of 1932 (Dimsdale, Horsewood, and Van Riel 2004: figure 1). Per capita income fell by a cumulative 18.9 percent between 1928 and 1932. Both crises intensified conflicts over economic policies, particularly unemployment compensation, as well as reviving disputes over payments of reparations.

German society was intensely polarized both over democracy and capitalism. The nationalistic Right developed an interpretation of German defeat in the war as being caused by the treason of socialists and democrats, a "stab in the back" (*Dochstosslegende*) rather than on the battlefields. The parties that accepted the conditions of the Armistice were dubbed "November criminals" by the nationalists. Anti-democratic thought of all kinds, not just Nazi, remained strong during the entire period (Sontheimer 1966). The Communist Party swung back and forth between purely insurrectionary and electoral strategies until 1928, when under the direction of the Comintern it adopted a "class contra class" posture, expecting that the economic crisis would mobilize the masses for a Communist revolution (Flechtheim 1966). The polarization was so intense that an eyewitness to these years observed that all one could ever hear was either "hooray" or "death to ... " (Haffner 2002: 57).

Successive governments were unstable and often unable to govern. Given the structure of political cleavages and the institutional system – most importantly, the electoral system – forming majority governments that were sufficiently homogeneous to be able to govern was next to impossible. The German electoral system was based on proportional representation without a threshold, leading to a proliferation of parties in the Reichstag, the parliament. While the election of 1919 was dominated by the Weimar Coalition and generated 4.1 effective parties, their number rose to 6.4 by 1920, 7.4 after the first election of 1924 and 6.2 after the second election the same year, 6.2 again in 1928, 7.1 in 1930, and when the Nazis became the plurality party, 4.3 in the first and 4.8 in the second election of 1932. The numbers of competing parties were bewildering: from eighteen in 1919 to twenty-six in 1920, twenty-nine in May 1924, twenty-eight in December 1924, forty-one in 1928, thirty-seven in 1930, sixty-two in July 1932, and sixty-one in November 1932. Yet until 1932 the SPD remained the plurality party. The German National People's Party (DNVP) was second or third until 1930, when it was passed by the Nazis and the KPD. The Zentrum was always third or fourth. The DDP (DStP as of 1930) and DVP (German People's Party) were also weakened by the progress of the Nazis and the KPD by 1930. Finally, the Bavarian People's Party (BVP, the Bavarian wing of the Zentrum) remained unaffected by all the changes, hovering at around twenty seats throughout the entire period. Hence, at least until 1930, the distribution of parliamentary seats was not particularly unstable. Government coalitions, however, were. Between February 11, 1919 and January 30, 1933, when Hitler became the *Reichskanzler*, the Weimar Republic experienced twenty-one cabinets, with an average duration of 243 days. The shortest was the second government of Stresemann in 1923, the longest was the broad coalition headed by Muller after the election of 1928.

Lepsius (1978: 41) places the parties on two dimensions: capitalist versus socialist and authoritarian versus democratic. His ranking on the pro-democracy dimension is

SPD and DDP, followed closely by Z+BVP, then at some distance DVP, DNVP, and KPD, and finally NSDAP (National Socialist German Workers' Party). His ranking on the pro-socialist dimension is KPD, SPD, in the center DDP, Z+BVP, and NSDAP, followed by DNVP, and then by DVP. The SPD was clearly committed to democracy and leftist on economic issues: its 1925 Heidelberg Program called for socialization of the means of production and its policies in the government promoted workers' rights and various social policies. The Zentrum and the DDP contained a broad range of economic positions; the DDP was resolutely democratic but the Zentrum contained some monarchists. The BVP, the Bavarian wing of the Zentrum, was more conservative and monarchist. The DVP was nationalistic, fiscally conservative, and lukewarm about democracy. The DNVP was nationalistic, somewhat less right-wing on economic issues than the DVP, anti-republican, and pro-monarchy. Note that Z, DVP, and DNVP moved to the right around 1930. The two parties never included in coalitions were the KPD and the NSDAP.

Figure 3.1 shows what the issue space may have looked like. If this mapping is correct, almost all of the coalitions were ideologically contiguous except for the Marx IV government (January 27, 1927 to June 28, 1928) that did not include the DDP, and the Brüning II coalition (September 15, 1930 to June 1, 1932) that did not include DVP. The center-left coalition, which included SPD, Z, and DDP, was alone never majoritarian after 1920. Neither was the center-right coalition of Z, DDP, and DVP (plus often BVP). Majoritarian coalitions would have to include SPD together with DVP, or Z and

44

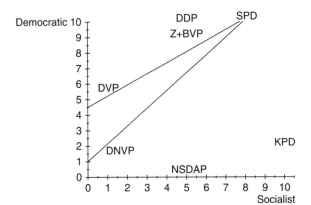

Figure 3.1. Putative location of parties on the Left–Right and democratic–authoritarian space
Parties: SPD (German Social Democratic Party), Z (Zentrum), DDP (German Democratic Party; changed name to DStP in 1930), DVP (German People's Party), BVP (Bavarian People's Party), DNVP (German National People's Party), NSDAP (National Socialist German Workers Party), KPD (German Communist Party)

DDP together with DNVP. The first of these coalitions was formed twice, under Stresemann I (August 13, 1923 to November 3, 1923) and Muller II (June 28, 1928 to March 29, 1930), but in both cases the SPD could not agree with the DVP over economic issues. The second was formed once, under Luther I (January 15, 1925 to October 26, 1925), but the DNVP left it over the Locarno Treaties. It seems that the distance between the SPD and the DVP was too large on economic issues and between Z and DNVP over nationalism, so that any majority coalition was too fragile to last an entire electoral period.

45

The parties themselves were far from homogeneous and disciplined. In particular, in several instances prime ministers found that they did not have the support of their own parties for the various policy compromises with which they attempted to save coalitions. This situation is best described by Lepsius (1978: 44; see also Carr 1969: 336): "The coherence of a government was achieved by the inter-action of a few personalities who could exert influence within their parties to make them tolerate the government from issue to issue . . . The government became more depen-dent on the prerogatives of the Reichspräsident and saw itself as an independent agency that had to continue govern-ing by continuous crisis management despite the fragmen-ted Parliament."

3. Signs.[1] German democracy emerged from the violence of World War I, and it emerged violent. From the outset, "political parties associated themselves with armed and uni-formed squads, paramilitary troops whose task it was to provide guards at meetings, impress the public by marching in military order through the streets, and to intimidate, beat up and on occasion kill members of the paramilitary units associated with other political parties. The relationship between the politicians and the paramilitaries was often fraught with tension, and paramilitary organizations always maintained a greater or lesser degree of autonomy; still, their political colouring was usually clear enough" (Evans 2003: KL 1707–11). Politically motivated murders were frequent:

---

[1] This subsection draws on Schumann (2009).

156 democratic politicians were assassinated by right-wing paramilitaries. Political violence peaked in 1923, with the bloody suppression of an abortive Communist uprising in Hamburg, gun battles between rival political groups in Munich, and armed clashes involving French-backed separatists in the Rhineland. While the period 1924–8 was relatively orderly and peaceful, social peace was shattered again by the crisis of 1929–30 and the subsequent rise of Nazi stormtroopers. "By the end of 1931," Carr (1969: 351) observes, "the centre of gravity of German political life was rapidly moving away from the Reichstag and the chancellery to the streets." According to Evans (2003, KL 5211–16),

> In 1930 the figures rose dramatically, with the Nazis claiming to have suffered seventeen deaths, rising to forty-two in 1931 and eighty-four in 1932. In 1932, too, the Nazis reported that nearly ten thousand of their rank-and-file had been wounded in clashes with their opponents. The Communists reported forty-four deaths in fights with the Nazis in 1930, 52 in 1931 and seventy-five in the first six months of 1932 alone, while over fifty Reichsbanner men died in battles with the Nazis on the streets from 1929 to 1933. Official sources broadly corroborated these claims, with one estimate in the Reichstag, not disputed by anybody, putting the number of dead in the year to March 1931 at no fewer than 300.

The summary of these events is shown in Figure 3.2, which illustrates the incidence of "unrest" (the number of events per year): again, the sum of riots, assassinations, general strikes, and anti-government demonstrations by year.

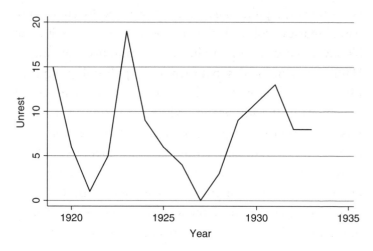

Figure 3.2. Unrest by year in Germany, 1919–33

The support for traditional parties, the top four vote-getters in 1919, eroded sharply over time, from their total share of 85.7 percent in 1919, to 68.3 in the first election of 1924, to 65.2 in 1928, to 51.6 in 1930, to 41.1 in the first election of 1930. Turnout fell from 83 percent in 1919 to 75.6 percent by 1928. Carr (1969: 337) observes that "interest in party politics was declining . . . Party politics – 'das System', as many started to call it – were clearly falling into disrepute." Yet the intensification of conflicts following the economic crisis resulted in turnout rising to 82 percent in 1930, when the Nazis brought previous non-voters to the polls. The number of voters increased from 31.2 million in 1928 to 35.2 million in 1930, while the number of votes for the NSDAP jumped from 810 thousand to 6.38 million. According to King et al. (2008), the main basis of support for the NSDAP was various kinds of self-employed, while people who were unemployed tended to vote Communist.

The extreme instability of economic, cultural, and political life of Weimar Germany made many people willing to embrace all kinds of delusions, including curing the sick by applications of cottage cheese or making gold from base metals. As another eyewitness reports, "The shock of Germany's defeat, the inflation, the get-rich-quick boom that followed stabilization, the influx of foreign money, and the swirl of underground activity against the 'internal and external enemy', had all combined to produce an atmosphere of unreality made to order for revivalists, quacks, and confidence men" (Delmer 1972: 95). Until 1930 Hitler was just one among many.

4. Outcome. The final outcome is known, so there is no point entering into details. Two aspects of Hitler's rise to office and the subsequent fall of democracy, however, merit emphasis. The first is that Hitler came to power legally, through an "authoritarian gap in the Weimar Constitution" (Bracher 1966: 119): Article 48 that allowed the president to empower the government to rule by decree. President Hindenburg used this prerogative in the winter of 1930, when the Reichstag could not agree on how to cope with the economic crisis and the coalition government led by the Social Democrat Muller resigned. Hindenburg appointed Heinrich Brüning as chancellor, making it clear that the new government could rely on emergency powers, and when Brüning could not muster a parliamentary majority in July 1930 he promulgated the budget by decree. From this point on, no government – Brüning's, Papen's, or Schleicher's – ruled with the support of a majority in the

Reichstag. The Reichstag lost its very raison d'être and almost ceased to meet: according to Evans (2003: KL 5328–30), "The Reichstag sat on average a hundred days a year from 1920 to 1930. It was in session for fifty days between October 1930 and March 1931; after that, it only met on twenty-four further days up to the elections of July 1932. From July 1932 to February 1933 it convened for a mere three days in six months." Hitler was appointed chancellor on January 30, 1933 with the same powers as his three predecessors. He grabbed dictatorial powers on March 23, 1933 when the Reichstag passed the "Law for the Relief of the People and the Reich" by the constitutionally required two-thirds majority, which allowed the government to issue decrees deviating from the constitution. While Communist deputies were not allowed to sit and some Social Democrats were too intimidated to participate, Hitler was still concerned about obtaining the requisite majority, which he did when the Zentrum voted in favor (Ermakoff 2008). Hence, from the purely legal point of view, the final coup against the Weimar Constitution was delivered constitutionally.

The second aspect of these events is that nobody – not the politicians who facilitated Hitler's entrance into the government, not his opponents, and seemingly not Hitler himself – expected him to monopolize and consolidate power. The NSDAP electoral success in 1930 was widely viewed as temporary and their reversal in the second election of 1932 as an indication that the Nazi tide was ebbing. After a Nazi defeat in a local election in 1932, an influential liberal newspaper proclaimed that "The mighty National

Socialist assault on the democratic state has been repulsed" (*Frankfurter Zeitung*, quoted in Turner 1985: 313). Moreover, by the second half of 1932 the Nazis were desperately short of money and Hitler was despondent about his chances of becoming chancellor. When Schleicher decided in 1932 to undermine Brüning and seek accommodation with Hitler, he was "assuming that it [the Nazi party] was a healthy nationalist movement which he could tame and exploit by adroit political manipulation" (Carr 1969: 352). Even when Hitler became chancellor, his cabinet included only three National Socialists as against eight non-Nazi conservatives. According to Delmer (1972: 117), the general perception was that "Hitler is Chancellor, but he is Chancellor in handcuffs. He is the prisoner of Papen, Hugenberg, and Hindenburg." Papen declared that "In less than two months we will have pushed Hitler so far into the corner that he'll be squeaking" (quoted in Bracher 1966: 120).

These two features of the events in Germany are worth retaining for general understanding of crises of democracy. The first is that particular institutional design matters: the proportional representation system made it difficult to form governments that could effectively govern, while the emergency powers embedded in the constitution permitted a constitutional slide into authoritarianism. The second is that the final outcome of these events was not foretold and not even anticipated by the people who ended up generating it. Contingency and the corresponding uncertainty are inherent aspects of complex conflicts.

3.2 Chile, 1970–1973

1. Democracy. The spell of democracy that ended in 1973 began in 1938, with the election of a Radical Party candidate Pedro Aguirre Cerda. The Communist Party was proscribed by President Gabriel González Videla in 1946, but the ban was overturned six years later by President Carlos Ibáñez del Campo. Partisan alternations in the presidency occurred in 1952, 1958, and 1964. In 1958, the winner, Jorge Alessandri, won the plurality of only 31.6 percent but his victory was recognized by the runner up, Salvador Allende. Hence, respect for results of elections was well entrenched.

2. Threats. By the mid-1960s, Chile was a country deeply divided along economic lines, with a wide spectrum of intensely held ideological beliefs about capitalism versus socialism. Political divisions based on class were profound. In 1958, 93 percent of "rich people" voted for the right-wing candidate, Alessandri, while 73 percent of workers voted for Allende (Prothro and Chaparro 1976: 73). Still, Navia and Osorno (2017) emphasize the importance of purely ideological divisions, autonomous from class positions. The importance of ideology is also documented by Prothro and Chaparro (1976: 87), who report that in the 1964 election, 59 percent of respondents gave purely ideological reasons for supporting or opposing Allende and 45 percent did the same for the winner, Eduardo Frei. While the evidence is only anecdotal, these divisions had deep roots in the social fabric, with gossip in Santiago about bourgeois fathers who expelled their

daughters from home not because they became pregnant but because they supported the Allende government.

Income inequality had been traditionally high in Chile. According to WIDER (UNU-WIDER 2014), the Gini of market incomes was 46.2 in 1964 and it increased to 50.3 by 1968 (50.5 according to SWIID), which was exceptionally high for this period. Labor share (from PWT9.0) was particularly low, at 45 percent. According to Lambrecht (2011), the highest decile received 40.23 percent of all incomes, while the lowest earned 1.45 percent. The upper 50 percent of recipients received 83 percent of national income, while the bottom 50 percent earned 17 percent. Distinguished by sector, 80.4 percent of people employed in agriculture were in the bottom half of recipients, 41.7 percent of those employed in industry, and 40.9 of those in services. By occupation, 72 percent of industrial workers received less than the median income and 89 percent of white-collar employees gained incomes higher than the median, while the self-employed were about equally likely to be in either bracket. In addition to the rural–urban cleavage, there were large differences across sectors: workers in copper mining and industry were much better off than the economically marginal groups that occupied newly formed Santiago slums, popularly called *callampas* ("mushrooms," because of how fast they grew). The reason for this high inequality was that the Chilean economy – industry, finance, and agriculture – was highly concentrated. In 1966, 144 firms owned more than 50 percent of industrial assets, three banks held 44.5 percent of deposits and received 55.1 percent of profits, while 9.7 percent of landowners owned 86 percent of cultivable land.

The crisis of governance, eventually a complete stale-mate between the president and the Congress, developed in steps. In the presidential election of September 4, 1970, the Left coalesced under the candidature of Dr. Salvador Allende, the Right was represented by Arturo Alessandri (PN), and the Christian Democrats (PDC) by a left-leaning candidate, Radomiro Tomic. The results were close, with Allende winning 36.1 percent, Alessandri 35 percent, and Tomic 28 percent. Given that no one won a majority, the final choice was to be made by the Congress. To stop Allende, some people around Alessandri were trying to craft a deal with the Christian Democrats, promising that if they voted for him, Alessandri would immediately resign, and that the outgoing Christian Democratic president, Eduardo Frei, who was eligible to run in the ensuing election, would win. Frei, however, refused to go along with this, so the deal collapsed. Alessandri himself called for the members of his party to vote for Allende, but the Executive Committee of the PN refused to follow his instruc-tion and Alessandri received thirty-five votes in the Congress. Allende was confirmed by the Congress on October 24 with the votes of seventy-eight members of his coalition and seventy-four Christian Democrats, assuming office on November 3.

Allende won by a small margin as the head of a coalition of seven parties, Unidad Popular (UP). This coali-tion included the center-left, represented by the Radical Party, which would split in June 1971; the Communist Party, which had a far-reaching program but was moderate and disciplined about tactics (Corvalan 2003); Allende's own Socialist Party; and several small groups, composed mainly of intellectuals (on divisions with the Left, see Yocelevzky 2002: chapter 2).

A radical Left extra-parliamentary group, the Movimiento de Izquierda Revolucionaria (MIR), rooted in the Santiago slums, remained outside the coalition. The original cabinet was composed of four Socialists, three Communists, three Radicals, two Social Democrats, two members of smaller parties, and one independent, who was the minister of the economy.

The new president inherited a House elected in 1969, in which the Christian Democrats held fifty-six seats, Partido Nacional thirty-four, the Communists twenty-two, the Radicals twenty-four, and the Socialists fifteen, of the total of 150. The composition of the Senate was similar. Hence, the government coalition held a minority of seats in both chambers and the Christian Democrats were pivotal.

To govern, Allende would have to find a compromise with the Christian Democrats that would be palatable to the members of his coalition. No such compromise would be found. Allende did not even control his own party: he had been proclaimed as the party's presidential candidate, with thirteen votes in favor and fourteen abstentions. The deeply divided Socialist Party took a sharp turn toward insurrectionary strategy in January 1971, when Carlos Altamirano replaced Aniceto Rodriguez as general secretary. Altamirano spoke in disparaging terms about the possibility of a "peaceful road to socialism," believing that because the bourgeoisie would defend its position by force, socialism could be achieved only by the armed action of the working class (Resolution of the Socialist Party adopted in la Serena in January 1971, Altamirano 1979: 19).

In addition to redistributive measures aimed at stimulating the economy in the short run, the program of the UP included continuing land distribution to peasants and completing the nationalization of copper, both initiated under the previous government, as well as nationalizing nitrate mining, banks, and some large industrial firms (see ODEPLAN 1971). Agrarian reform had already been enabled by a law passed under Eduardo Frei in 1969. Copper was nationalized by a unanimous vote in the Congress, while other mining sectors and the banks were gradually bought by the state, with the opposition of their United States and Chilean owners, but without requiring legislation. The nationalization of industrial firms, however, required a law. Note that while some sectors of the UP coalition pushed for nationalization as a goal in itself, the government portrayed it as limited and instrumental. The minister of the economy, Pedro Vukovic, argued that given the highly oligopolist structure of the Chilean economy and the endemically high inflation, the state should take over one or two large firms in each of the crucial sectors, and use pricing by these firms as an instrument to control inflation.

The government negotiated an agreement with the Christian Democrats, with vague criteria – "firms that operated activities of primary importance for the economic life of the country" – according to which firms would be nationalized, moved to mixed ownership, or remain private. On October 12, 1971, the government sent to the Congress a bill that would implement this agreement, *La Ley de las Areas*. On the eve of the vote, however, a split within the Christian Democratic Party led it to renege on the original agreement, substituting the original bill by a law that would allow the Congress to decide each nationalization one-by-one. While the original goal of the government was to nationalize 243 firms, later scaled down to ninety-one, it was estimated that the Congress could process with at most eight nationalizations per year (Martner 1988). This law was passed by both houses of the Congress on February 19, 1972. It included annulling 520 expropriations made after October 14, 1971. Following a massive demonstration by the Left against this version of the reform, Allende vetoed it on April 11, 1972, and the opposition, led by the president of the Senate, Patricio Aylwin, demonstrated against the veto the day after. The result was a legal limbo. Under pressure from several members of the UP as well as from ordinary workers, Allende reverted to an obscure and never previously used decree dating to 1932, according to which the state could intervene in firms "paralyzed by labor unrest." Needless to say, workers in many firms, including small family-held enterprises, were only too eager to paralyze them and have the state intervene. The result was chaos, which turned out to be uncontrollable. By October 1972, workers occupied several Santiago factories. Spontaneous forms of self-organization, *Cordones Industriales* and *Comandos Comunales*, emerged to replace formal economic and state organizations (for details, see de Vylder 1974: chapter 6).

Once the *Ley de las Areas* failed, the executive–legislative stalemate was complete. To the best of my knowledge, not a single major bill proposed by the government was subsequently passed by the Congress and all major laws passed by the Congress were vetoed by the president. In a Chilean tradition dating back to the early twentieth century, the Congress raised constitutional accusations and censored several ministers, to which Allende's reaction was always to change their portfolios and keep them. By September 1, 1972, Senator Hamilton (PDC) called for the resignation of the president and the clamor for impeachment became frequent. Impeachment, however, required a two-thirds majority, which the opposition could not muster in the parliamentary elections of March 1973, when Allende still enjoyed the support of 49.7 percent of survey respondents in Santiago (Navia and Osorio 2017).

The final constitutional limbo emerged late in 1972. On October 23, 1972 the Congress passed a law which granted the armed forces the prerogative to search all places that may store arms and explosives, which according to the opposition were being secretly amassed by some pro-government organizations. The president responded by invoking a legal clause according to which the armed forces had no right to enter public buildings without his specific authorization. Up to this time, the position of most leading generals was that the armed forces should remain apolitical unless the government violated the constitution. This conflict, however, rendered the criterion of constitutionality inoperative. On August 22, 1973, the Congress declared that the government violated the constitution and was illegitimate. One day later General Pinochet replaced General Prats as the head of the armed forces, and the road was opened to the coup of September 11.

3. Signs.[2] As soon as Allende was elected, the Right initiated a US-assisted "campaign of terror," raising the specter of Soviet domination. On October 22, 1970, a group of officers aiming to generate political instability attempted to kidnap

---

[2] The chronology in this subsection is based mainly on Los mil dias de Allende (1997).

the head of the armed forces, General Schneider, but ended up killing him.

Conflicts in agriculture and strikes in industry intensified immediately after the election. While in 1969, the last year of Frei's government, there were 1,127 strikes in the countryside and 148 instances in which peasants occupied *latifundia* ("tomas de fundo"), in 1970 there were 1,580 strikes and 456 occupations, of which 192 took place in the last three months of 1970 alone (Landsberger and McDaniel 1976). According to a different source (Martner 1988), there were 1,758 rural strikes in 1971, while occupations increased from 450 in 1970 to 1,278 in 1971. Both the president and the minister of agriculture spoke publicly against illegal land seizures, but could not control them. Landowners mobilized, in some cases importing arms, and organized forcible retakings of land. They created para-judicial institutions, *Tribunales Agrarios*, that ruled in their favor. Owners who earlier had ceded land when it was legally expropriated joined in the resistance.

In 1969 there were 977 industrial and mining strikes with 275,000 workers participating; in 1971, the first full year of Allende, there were 2,709 strikes involving 302,000 workers; and in 1972 there were 3,289 strikes engaging 397,000 workers. Note that the strikes extended to smaller firms, as indicated by the ratio of strikers to strikes.

The Right first occupied the streets on December 1, 1971, when elite women of Santiago marched banging empty pots (*cacerolas vacias*), protected by bodyguards from a fascist group, *Patria y Libertad*. They were attacked with stones by a Left counter-demonstration. Ten months later, in October 1972, the country was paralyzed by a strike of truck owners, lockout of many factories, and work stoppage by professionals. To deal with the unrest a state of emergency was declared by the government, and in November the military entered the government for the first time, with General Prats becoming the minister of interior. Another strike of truck owners took place in August 1973.

The violence escalated from the first shooting on December 2, 1970, when two left-wing students were wounded in Concepción. A peasant was killed during a land occupation on June 9, 1971. The assassination of General Schneider was followed by the murder, also on June 9, by an obscure left-wing group (VOP, *Vanguardia Organizada del Pueblo*) of a former minister of interior, Edmundo Pérez Zujovic. A few days later two members of the VOP were killed in a five-hour shoot-out with the police. By October 28, 1971 *El Mercurio* reported seven armed confrontations during land conflicts in Temuco, with four dead and nineteen wounded. Another conflict over land ended with one person dead and three wounded on November 22, 1971. On May 20, 1972 the shootings moved to Santiago, with a member of MIR killed by the police. A violent conflict between inhabitants of a Santiago slum and the police led to one dead and several wounded on August 5, 1972. Street fighting took place over the government's education bill, with several wounded, on April 26, 1973. Allende's military aide, Arturo Araya, was murdered by *Patria y Libertad* on June 27, 1973. By mid-June 1973, shootings, explosions, and fires became daily occurrences: supermarkets were sacked, right-wing paramilitary groups fired shots from cars and exploded bombs at several local headquarters of

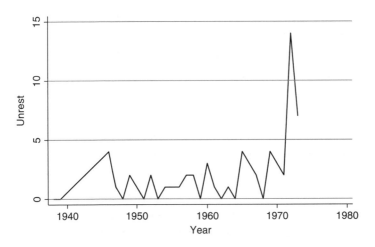

Figure 3.3. Unrest by year in Chile, 1938–73

government parties, and workers from the El Teniente mine marched to Santiago behind a tractor filled with explosives (Bitar and Pizarro no date). The government tried to find a far-reaching accommodation with the opposition, the Catholic Church tried to mediate, but the spiral of violence could not be stopped.

As Figure 3.3 shows, the incidence of popular unrest skyrocketed in 1972. None of these dramatic events affected the distribution of political attitudes. In 1972, 99 percent of upper-income respondents said that household staples are "difficult" to find, while 75 percent of lower-income persons found it "easy." Surveys reported by Prothro and Chaparro (1976: 102 and 104) show that both the upper and lower class agreed that Chile was "living in a climate of violence," but only 7 percent of upper-income respondents attributed it exclusively to the opposition while 35 percent of lower-income respondents did. The vote shares of the five largest parties in the congressional elections in March 1973 remained almost the same as in 1969, with a slight gain for the Socialists. Turnout was higher in 1973 than in 1969, while the potential electorate increased by almost 40 percent. Hence, there were no signs either of dissatisfaction with party politics or of erosion of support for the traditional parties.

The most ominous signals emanated from the military. While the official stand of the military leadership was that the armed forces would stay away from politics as long as the government did not violate the constitution, officers impatient to depose the government by force were many. General Viaux, who commanded the operation against General Schneider in October 1970, had already led a mutiny over military pay against President Frei in 1969. A failed coup attempt of June 1973 was led by a lower-ranking officer, Colonel Souper. Throughout the entire period, the possibility of a coup led by some group of the military was the most frequently discussed topic in Santiago. After the Right failed to obtain the two-thirds of the seats required to impeach the president, in the election of March 1973, it became clear that Christian Democrats, by then led by the future democratic president of Chile, Patricio Aylwin, would welcome a coup. By July of 1973, the only question was what form the coup would assume. The fear was that if it were initiated by a navy unit stationed in the south of the country it would lead to a civil war, but most people expected a *golpe blando*, in which the military leadership would put Allende on a plane to Cuba and call for an election that would be won by Eduardo Frei. I do not know anyone who expected that the coup would be as ferocious and bloody as it eventually turned out to be, or that the military would stay in power for sixteen years.

4. Outcome. As Hutchison, Klubock, and Milanic (2013: 348) remarked, "The tensions between the phased and controlled revolution from above and the more spontaneous and locally informed revolution from below were never resolved, constituting a fatal flaw in the Chilean revolutionary process." One major aspect of the dynamic of Chilean events was the inability of the government to control its own supporters. Allende could not act strategically because groups within his own party as well as some other members of his coalition, notably excluding Communists, could not be disciplined to moderate their demands and to demobilize when the situation so required. Lord Bevan, a minister in the UK's postwar Labour government, once remarked that "We do not want to be in the position of having to listen to our own people." Allende did not have this choice: peasants were occupying land against the pleading of the government, some sectors of the coalition were amassing arms against the injunction by the government, and an important leftwing armed group was not even a member of the governing coalition. Ideological passion was intense, discipline nonexistent.

The Chilean events again highlight the importance of the democratic institutional framework. In contrast to Weimar, Chile had a purely presidential system. Under this system a government can become paralyzed when different political forces control the executive and the legislature: "divided government" in the parlance of the United States. Legislation initiated by the executive was not passed by the legislature; legislation passed by the Congress was vetoed by the president. When the paralysis became acute, the president sought emergency powers while the Congress moved to impeach the president. In the meantime, incomes were falling, inflation soared, and shortages became ubiquitous, while the supporters of the opposite camps tried to impose themselves on the streets.

Finally, the Chilean events speak to the tension between democracy and capitalism. Writing in 1886, Hjalmar Branting, the leader of the Swedish Social Democrats, wondered whether "the upper class would respect popular will even if it demanded the abolition of its privileges" (quoted in Tingsten 1973: 361). An SPD leader, August Bebel, thought in 1905 that revolution may be necessary "as a purely defensive measure, designed to safeguard the exercise of power legitimately acquired through the ballot" (quoted in Schorske 1955: 43). Clearly, Allende did not have a popular mandate for far-reaching social and economic transformations: he won the presidency by a slim plurality and his coalition never had a majority in the legislature. He did win according to the rules and tried to govern according to the rules, but he was being pushed by the forces behind him to reach beyond his mandate. The upper class, whose privileges were being threatened, turned to the military and, not without some hesitation, the military were willing to oblige.

3.3 France, 1954–1962 and 1968

1. Democracy. The French Third Republic was founded in 1875. Elections were held regularly until 1939, with control

64

over government changing partisan hands nine times during this period. In the immediate aftermath of World War II a series of provisional governments, the first headed by General Charles de Gaulle and the last by Leon Blum, governed the country until a new constitution was adopted in 1946, giving birth to the Fourth Republic. Parliamentary elections were held under this constitution in November 1946, June 1951, and January 1956.

2. Threats. The first years after the war witnessed a high degree of social unrest, culminating in 1947 with a series of insurrectionary strikes, which were bloodily repressed. A massive strike of the public sector took place in 1953 but there were no more major labor conflicts during the remaining years of the Fourth Republic, until May 1958.

From 1946 France was engaged in several colonial wars against independence movements. The Indochina war ended in July 1954 after the rout of the French forces at Dien Bien Phu. However, a few months later a new war began in Algeria, with profound consequences for the next eight years. This war, which until 1999 was officially referred to euphemistically as "the Algerian events," caused deep divisions within French society and several rifts between civilian authorities and the army units stationed in Algeria, with two coup attempts, in May 1958 and in April 1961, as well as a wave of terrorism.

Government instability and ineffectiveness under the Fourth Republic mirrored that of Weimar Germany. The electoral law adopted in 1945 (in France electoral laws are not a part of the constitution) provided for proportional representation at the level of electoral districts. This law was slightly modified in 1951 to allow electoral coalitions and to introduce a dose of majoritarianism, with the intention to reduce the weight of the Communists and the Gaullists (Bon 1978: 68). Between January 22, 1947 and June 2, 1958, twenty-four governments were in office, for an average duration of 173 days, shorter than the 243 in Weimar, ranging from two days to one year and four months. Moreover, between October 27, 1946 and June 2, 1958, there were 375 days, more than one year in twelve, during which there were no governments. All the governments of the Fourth Republic were coalitions of several parties, from four to eight. After Paul Ramadier, the first prime minister of the Fourth Republic, expelled the Communists (PCF) from his government in October 1947, continuity during the term of the parliament elected in 1946 was provided by the presence in all the ten governments of three parties: SFIO (Socialist), MRP (Radical), and PRS (Radical-Socialist). The last two parties also participated in all governments following the election of June 17, 1951, but the SFIO was not included in any of the eight governments in office during this term. The parliament was dissolved at the end of 1955, with the election following on January 2, 1956, and the SFIO joined all the subsequent governments of the Fourth Republic. The fragility of the successive governments made them incapable of making major decisions, while the continuity of their composition meant that no other political alignment constituted a viable alternative. As Denquin (1988: 88) observes, "From the point of view of citizens, the political system was lived as at the same time odious and natural."

3. Signs. None of the short-lived governments was able to build majority consensus over the handling of the Algerian

conflict. The Mendes France government's plan of reforms was defeated in the *Assemblée* and it resigned on March 3, 1955. The succeeding government of Edgar Faure proclaimed a state of emergency in Algeria but did not survive either. The combination of the intensification of the Algerian crisis with the incapacity of the successive governments to cope with it made attempts at forming governments increasingly frantic. When the government of Guy Mollet (SFIO), which granted special powers to the military in Algeria, fell on May 21, 1957, the interregnum lasted three weeks. It was followed by the government of Maurice Bourgès-Maunoury (PRS), which lasted 110 days. After this government fell on September 30, 1957, two attempts to form a government, by Antoine Pinay (CNIP) and by Guy Mollet, failed, and the next government was formed only on November 6. This government, headed by Félix Gaillard (PRS), proposed a new framework law for Algeria, which was again defeated in the parliament, and the government resigned after 160 days in office. It took twenty-nine days to form the next government, of Pierre Pflimin (MRP), which lasted fourteen days. Altogether, the fall of Mollet was followed by eighty-nine days in which France had no government. The last government of the Fourth Republic was formed by General Charles de Gaulle on June 1, 1958.

Interpretations of de Gaulle's accession to the office of prime minister are highly controversial. It would be presumptuous for me to take a side in this controversy, which centers on the issue of whether de Gaulle was complicit in the events that brought him to power. The basic facts, however, are known. On May 13, 1958, several groups of civilians assaulted and occupied the seat of government in Algiers, with the passive attitude of the police forces that were guarding it. The leaders of the insurrection, some but not all of whom were Gaullists, formed a Committee of Public Safety, headed by an active general, Jacques Massu, and declared that they would govern Algeria until a government favorable to maintaining French control over the colony was installed in Paris. The intention of the insurrection was to prevent the investiture of Pflimin and force on the *Assemblée* the candidature of de Gaulle. On May 24, a similar Committee of Public Safety was formed in Corsica, so it appeared that the revolt was spreading toward the metropolis (*Operacion Ressurection*). Pflimin was named prime minister on May 14, but on May 27 de Gaulle broke his silence, declaring himself a candidate for the office, and ordering the military in Algeria to obey the orders of their superiors. The declaration certainly reads like a usurpation of powers the general did not yet have: "In these conditions, all actions by whatever side that undermine public order risk to have serious consequences. While recognizing the circumstances, I will not approve them" (quoted in Denquin 1988: 171). The Pflimin government resigned one day later and the parliament invested a government headed by de Gaulle. It was a broad coalition of six parties plus independents and it included three former prime ministers. The government was granted the power to rule by decrees for six months and to initiate the project of a new constitution. Hence, while the procedure by which de Gaulle acceded to office was constitutional, his advent to power was a response to a coup d'état in Algeria as well as the opening gambit on his part.

The project of the new constitution was prepared rapidly. First, however, the parliament had to modify the amendment clause of the Constitution of the Fourth Republic, Article 90, to allow the change of the entire constitution. Having done this, the new government subjected the constitutional project to a referendum. Before voting, each household received two ballots (yes or no?), the text of the constitution, and the text of a speech by de Gaulle of September 4, arguing for the new constitution. The constitution was supported by 79 percent of voters in the metropolis and 95 percent in Algeria. It was formally adopted on September 28, 1958 and de Gaulle was elected president on December 21, 1958, with Michel Debré becoming prime minister. The law regulating parliamentary elections was changed by a decree of the government on October 13, 1958.

The new president's views on the solution to the Algerian crisis are again subject to conflicting interpretations, namely, whether he believed from the outset that the independence of Algeria was inevitable or changed his views as events unfolded. In the immediate aftermath of his accession to office, in a famous speech in which he told the French in Algeria, "Je vous écoute" ("I hear you"), he let it be understood that he favored the colonial status quo, *Algérie Française*, albeit accompanied by the extension of political rights to Algerians and massive investment projects to develop the territory. Yet his stance evolved rapidly, causing French Algerians to claim that they were being betrayed. Public opinion in France was evolving as well: in July 1956, 45 percent of respondents were favorable to negotiations with "chiefs of the rebellion," in July 1957 the proportion was 53 percent, in May 1959 it rose to 71 percent

(Ageron 1976). As de Gaulle's language was shifting from "association," to "autodetermination," and then to "Algérie algérienne," conflicts erupted within the French community in Algeria. Violent Franco–Franco confrontation took place on February 24, 1960, with several deaths. On June 16, 1960 an organization defending French Algeria (*Front Algérie Française*, FAF) was formed; it engaged in several violent demonstrations, and was banned in December of that year. A referendum on autodetermination, which took place on January 8, 1961, was supported by 75.8 percent in the metropolis and 69.1 percent in Algeria. A terrorist organization, *Organisation Armée Secrète*, that was to engage in many bombings and several assassinations, was formed in February 1961. On April 22, 1961, several generals proclaimed the secession of Algeria from France, under their government. According to Droz and Lever (1991: 296–313), this new attempt at a coup generated feverish fears in Paris of an impending invasion, but it fizzled out when the army recruits refused to obey the rebellious generals. The agreement to end the war was concluded on March 19, 1962, and it was ratified by the referendum of April 8, 1962.

The economic, social, and military burden of the war was enormous: altogether 1.75 million Frenchmen served in Algeria, of whom 1.34 million were conscripts. It deeply divided French society, not only in Algeria but also in the metropolis, with several instances in which police bloodily repressed antiwar demonstrations. After several protestors were killed on February 8, 1962, their funeral brought 500,000 people to the streets.

4. Outcome. The Algerian war was a disaster that could not be coped with by any government under the institutional framework of the Fourth Republic. Yet, even if the war continued for another four years, the impasse was broken by the advent of de Gaulle to office, the broad powers granted to him, and the institutional change that moved the center of power from the parliament to the president.

Forget all the details and consider the situation in abstract terms. A society is experiencing a profound disaster and the institutional framework does not generate governments that could effectively cope with it. The military rises in arms to affect the orientation of a new government. A retired general, a war hero, takes the initiative of imposing himself as the head of the government. He demands, and obtains from the parliament, the power to rule by decree and to change the constitution. His government controls the press and the radio, bans several organizations on both sides of the conflict, and prosecutes several people for "demoralizing the army" (Denquin 1988: 150). The story sounds familiar, and ominous. Yet eventually the war ends and democracy survives.

In the aftermath of World War II, the anti-democratic forces, mainly former supporters of the Vichy regime, were weak in France. They opposed de Gaulle from the Right but all the organized political forces were resolutely democratic. This commitment was enshrined in Article 93 of the 1946 constitution, which stated that the one aspect of the constitution that could not be amended was the republican form of government. The rebellious military were prepared to engage in insurrectionary activities but their demands were restricted to keeping

Algeria French, not to instituting an authoritarian regime. Indeed, many of the military rebels were Gaullist. There are, thus, good reasons to think that any attempt at installing a dictatorship would have been violently opposed. But the story of 1958 cannot be told without invoking the personality of General de Gaulle. While not hesitating to use all the instruments of power, including highly repressive ones, to lead France through the labyrinth of the war, de Gaulle never thought to establish a lasting dictatorship. Indeed, when the opposition raised in May 1958 the specter of de Gaulle becoming a dictator, he responded: "Would one believe that, at the age of 67, I will begin a career of a dictator?"

He did not. In 1962 the constitution was amended to allow for the direct election of the president. Yet in 1965, de Gaulle was humiliated by failing to be elected in the first round of the presidential election, even if he was re-elected with 55.2 percent of the vote in the second round. Four years later, on April 28, 1969, he resigned from office after a defeat in a minor referendum. The institutions of the Fifth Republic survived his departure from office and his erstwhile opponent, François Mitterrand, became president in 1981.

The first lesson of the French crisis is again institutional: given the relations of political forces, no government formed under the institutions of the Fourth Republic was able to muster the majority required to act decisively in the face of a disaster.

This situation was remedied by the constitutional change, which strengthened the power of the chief executive and stabilized the governments. The temporary powers granted to the newly elected president were almost unlimited, yet he was willing and probably compelled to tolerate opposition and thus to preserve democracy. Counterfactual questions again highlight the role of contingencies: What would have happened had someone with personal authority over the military not been available to become a civilian leader? What would have happened had the leader been willing to use his constitutionally acquired powers to eradicate the democratic opposition? Such questions are unanswerable, but they demonstrate that the survival of democracy in France may have been a historical accident, as was its failure in Nazi Germany.

5. A note on May 1968. The French events of May 1968 were dramatic but I do not think that they threatened democracy. They were certainly violent: some thousands of people were injured, including 1,912 among the police forces (Le Gac, Olivier, and Spina 2015: 524). Yet with millions of people on the streets, massive strikes, barricades, and occupations of buildings, the death toll was minimal (between four and seven). No significant terrorist groups emerged in the aftermath. Even if there were some dramatic moments, the situation was quickly stabilized when the government overwhelmingly won the parliamentary elections of June 23–30, 1968.

To complete the story, Figure 3.4 shows the incidence of unrest in France between 1945 and 1970, with the peaks in 1947, 1960–4, and 1968.

3.4 United States, 1964–1976

1. Democracy. The oldest democracy in the world, the United States experienced several crises, most profoundly

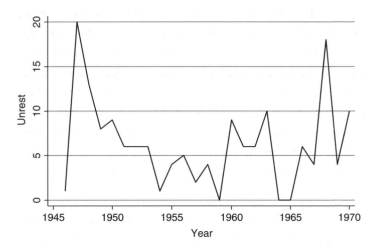

Figure 3.4. Unrest by year in France, 1945–70

the Civil War. Waves of repression occurred intermittently: during the Civil War, in the aftermath of World War I, and during and after World War II. Yet even the most bloody war in history did not interrupt the regular functioning of representative institutions: all elections occurred on schedule and the Congress never ceased to function.

2. Threats. Civil strife was widespread during the 1960s, principally in the form of urban riots (Rochester, Harlem, Philadelphia in 1964; Watts in 1965; Cleveland, Omaha in 1966; Newark, Plainfield, Detroit, Minneapolis in 1967; Chicago, Washington, Baltimore, Cleveland in 1968). Two political assassinations, of Martin Luther King and of Robert Kennedy, occurred in 1968. The country was embroiled in the Vietnam War, which was highly divisive

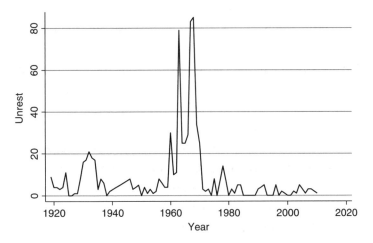

Figure 3.5. Unrest by year in United States, 1919–2012

internally. Mass demonstrations against the war began in 1964 and continued throughout the period. Repression was widespread. In 1966, the House Committee on Un-American Activities launched investigations into the opponents of the war. On May 4, 1970, the National Guard opened fire on students demonstrating against the war at Kent State University, killing four and wounding twelve demonstrators, while a few weeks later the police killed two students and injured twelve at Jackson State University. As Figure 3.5 shows, incidence of unrest was high during the 1960s, culminating in 1968.

3. Signs. Richard Nixon was elected the 37th President of the United States in 1968, and while the electoral campaign was punctuated by violence, notably the "police

riot" during the 1968 Chicago Democratic Convention, his first term showed no signs of a crisis of democratic institutions. As the election of 1972 approached, however, Nixon began to use government agencies for partisan purposes. He ordered surveillance of his potential opponent, Senator Ted Kennedy. An "enemies list," with expanding membership, was made by his staff, with the purpose of targeting those on it using federal agencies. One of his counsels, John Dean, made the purpose of this list clear: "This memorandum addresses the matter of how we can maximize the fact of our incumbency in dealing with persons known to be active in their opposition to our Administration; stated a bit more bluntly – how we can use the available federal machinery to screw our political enemies" (memorandum by John Dean to Lawrence Higby, August 16, 1971). The targeted enemies were bugged and the Federal Bureau of Investigation, the Central Intelligence Agency, and the Internal Revenue Service were utilized to harass them. The operative unit coordinating this campaign was the Committee for Reelection of the President, popularly nicknamed CREEP. Nixon was re-elected in 1972, but as news of the bungled burglary of the Democratic National Committee in June 1972 was becoming public, the campaign by the administration against the media and the courts intensified. Even though the Vietnam War ended on January 27, 1973, the Watergate scandal continued to embroil people around the president in violations of legality. The commitment of the Nixon administration to defend its power by all means is evidenced by the fact that sixty-nine of his supporters were eventually charged and forty-eight were convicted of illegal acts related to the Watergate scandal, including two attorney generals, the chief of staff, three White House staffers, the secretary of commerce, and Nixon's personal lawyer.

4. Outcome. The remarkable aspect of the crisis in the United States is that the representative institutions, the system of checks and balances, worked effectively to stop the abuse of power by the president. The Senate voted seventy-seven to zero to open the investigation of the Watergate incident and subsequently the House initiated impeachment procedures against the president. It is important to note that both houses were controlled by the Democrats. Yet some Republican senators and representatives also voted against the president. Courts also played a role in the development of the crisis: the decision of the Supreme Court to force Nixon to release his tapes brought the administration to the precipice. Facing the prospect of inevitable impeachment, President Nixon resigned on August 8, 1976.

The obvious counterfactual question is whether the institutional system would have counteracted the abuse of power by the president had Republicans controlled both houses of Congress. Does the system of checks and balances work, as James Madison had hoped, because members of different institutions defend the interests of their institutions, or only if the powers of the government are divided between different parties and the representatives defend their partisan interests?

4

Lessons from History: What to Look For

Such absolute certainties have eluded me. I have found only a series of ups and downs and a succession of unforeseeable contingencies, none of which seem to have been inevitable.

(Alon 2002: 11, about Weimar Germany)

If the past illuminates, the future depends on whether the conditions we observe at the present mirror those of the past. Hence, it is still premature to draw lessons. The past tells us, however, what we should be looking for, what the signs are that a democracy is in crisis and what kinds of events may actually lead to its downfall.

If the past is a guide, we should be looking at economic conditions: income, its growth, and its distribution. We should consider the democratic history of a particular country: how entrenched democracy is in terms of the habit of changing governments through elections. We should pay attention to the intensity of divisions in society: both the extent of political polarization and of hostility between adherents of different political solutions.

All the four cases in Chapter 3 indicate that we should also pay attention to the particular forms of democratic institutions, in particular to whether they are conducive to the formation of majority governments that can act decisively if some disasters occur, yet without being able to usurp power. Yet making counterfactual inferences is perilous. Would democracy have survived in Germany under institutions more favorable to stable majority governments? Would the Chilean coup have been avoided under a parliamentary system, in which the chief executive could be removed by institutional procedures? As much as political scientists believe in the importance of institutions, perhaps the conflicts in these two countries were just too intense to be peacefully managed under any institutional arrangement.

Clearly, these directives are biased by what we can observe. The intuitions from memoirs and even novels may be as illuminating as from systematic data: they tell us how individuals perceived and experienced the dramatic events in which they were protagonists and, in the end, it is their actions that determined the outcomes of crises.

Conditions do not determine the outcomes; actions of people under the conditions do. Even when the conditions are given, outcomes are not unique. For example, Stern (1966: xvii) thinks that "By 1932, the collapse of Weimar had become inevitable; the triumph of Hitler had not." But perhaps by 1925 even the fall of the Republic was not inevitable: had the KPD or the Bavarian People's Party (BVP) voted for the Zentrum candidate, Marx, in the second round of the presidential elections, Hindenburg with his anti-democratic instincts would not have been there in 1932 and who knows what would have happened. One can entertain similar fantasies about Chile: after the change of leadership of the Christian Democrats resulting in the rejection of the Ley de las Areas, perhaps the fall of Allende was inevitable but the brutal coup was not. Conversely, one may wonder what would have happened in France had a leader with impeccable military

79

credentials not been available or not been a democrat. I do not think that we can answer such questions, so we must allow that the lessons from history are paltry, and that the future is not uniquely determined by present conditions – that it is uncertain.

Part II

The Present: What Is Happening?

A candidate claiming to be a billionaire, who advocates lowering taxes and reducing social programs, is supported by the working class, while a candidate who wants to tax the rich is supported by the *Wall Street Journal*. A thrice-married man who prides himself on unwanted sexual advances receives almost unanimous support from religious groups committed to "family values." A lot of people believe any kind of apparent nonsense. The incumbent party loses an election when the economy is the best it's been in recent decades. An election in which almost all parties, including the victorious one, campaign against "the establishment" generates a parliament that is even more elitist than the outgoing one. A blow against globalization, the free flow of capital and commodities, is inflicted by parties on the right wing of the political spectrum. Nationalists form international alliances. None of this makes sense.

What is going on and why? What do we need to make sense of if we suspect that democracy may be in crisis? I want to make sense of the current political, economic, social, and cultural transformations: what, if anything, do they add up to? Yet "making sense" is a deceptive endeavor, guided by what Pangloss tells us in Voltaire's *Candide*: that there must be a "because" for everything, everything must be logically connected. As intellectuals, we seek hidden logical connections among appearances: in Marx's words, "If essence and appearance coincided, no science would be necessary." But the danger is that we may overdo it, finding causal connections where none exist. While the quest for sense is inexorable, finding it is always perilous: our beliefs are replete with false positives.

Moreover, it is not always obvious of what we should be making sense, what are the "facts." As Leo Goodman once said, "A fact in fact is quite abstract." Facts are constructed, subject to interpretation, and often disputed. Which parties should be considered to be radical Right? Does automation reduce the demand for labor or are jobs that are substituted by machines replaced by other jobs? Is there a "hollowing of the middle class"? What is the marginal product of the CEOs? Not only explanations but even facts cannot be taken for granted.

In what follows, I invert the schema used to analyze the past. I first describe the signs that a crisis may be here: the collapse of traditional parties, the rise of the radical Right, and of attitudes supporting it. Then I venture into possible explanations: economic, cultural, and autonomously political. Subsequently, I address the issues entailed in looking for causality and focus on micro-level explanations. Finally, I ask whether and which of the current conditions may be historically unprecedented and ominous.

5

The Signs

The signs that we may be experiencing a crisis include: (1) the rapid erosion of traditional party systems; (2) the rise of xenophobic, racist, and nationalistic parties and attitudes; and (3) the decline in support for "democracy" in public opinion surveys.

5.1 Erosion of Traditional Party Systems

Party systems that endured without much change during almost a century are eroding in many countries. The systems that emerged in Western European and Anglo-Saxon countries in the aftermath of World War I were typically dominated by two parties, one left and one right of center. Parties bearing social democratic, socialist, or labor labels occupied the space of the moderate Left. The labels were more varied on the Right, but each country had at least one major party located right of center. These systems have remained almost ossified until recently. While at times they changed labels, merging and splitting, they survived not only the turmoil of the interwar period and World War II but also the profound economic, demographic, and cultural transformations of more than fifty years following the war.

However we characterize this stability, it is astonishing.[1] Very few parties that did not receive at least 20 percent of the

---

[1] The following numbers and figures are based on countries that were members of the OECD as of 2000, except for Greece, Italy, Portugal, and

vote in the elections closest to 1924 have broken this barrier since. Liberals in 1929 in the United Kingdom and NSDAP in 1932 in Germany were the only ones to do so before 1939. The immediate aftermath of World War II witnessed an upsurge of the Left vote (Communist in France in 1945, Finnish People Democratic League in 1945, Socialist in Japan in 1947). Between 1951 and 1978 only two parties, in Belgium and in France, crossed for the first time the threshold of 20 percent. Yet from 1978 until the moment this text is being written seventeen new parties broke this barrier. One way to see this stability and its erosion is that, in spite of the upheaval following World War II, a new party crossed the threshold once every 7.6 years between 1924 and 1977 and once every 2.3 years after 1977.

Another way to characterize this stability and its erosion is to consider the percent of the two top vote-getters in each country around 1924 that remained in the top two in the subsequent elections. Except for NSDAP in 1930, the two top vote-getters remained in this position in all the countries under consideration during the entire period until 1945. The aftermath of the war shook their positions somewhat, but almost 90 percent of the two 1924 leaders remained in the top two until the late 1990s. A major destabilization in 1999 was largely overcome by 2007, but the 2008 financial crisis led to another major shake-up. Chiaramonte and Emanuele (2017) show that the movement of voters across parties has

Spain. The total number of countries is nineteen. Given the changes of names, mergers, and splits it is sometimes necessary to make decisions about which parties are heirs of the already existing ones and which are new. The data cover the period through 2014.

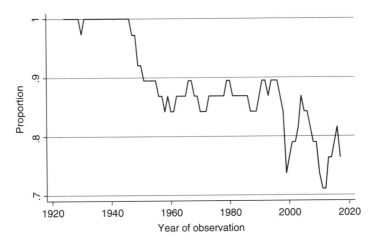

Figure 5.1. Proportion of parties that were the two top vote winners around 1924 that remained in the top two

increased in the most recent period and that electoral volatility is due mainly to the entry and exit of parties. Figure 5.1 illustrates these patterns.

This picture still underestimates the original stability as well as its recent erosion. It underestimates the stability because several countries had a three- or even four-party system in which the vote margins between the parties were small, so that it was easy for them to change places. But considering only party labels, rather than their programs, does not take into account the general ideological drift to the right, both of the center-left and the center-right parties (see Maravall 2016). If we were to consider programs, the recent destabilization would appear more pronounced.

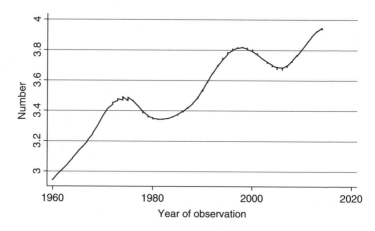

Figure 5.2. Effective number of parties in the electorate since
1960, in countries that were members of the OECD as of 2000
Source: Armigeon et al. 2016 CDPS Lowess smooth

Finally, as Figure 5.2 shows, the effective number of
parties[2] in the electorate has increased since the early 1980s,
again with an upturn during the past few years.

All these trends indicate that the traditional party systems are crumbling. But an argument can be made that this is
not a sign of a crisis but just a routine partisan realignment that
will result in a rejuvenation of democracy. Hopefully we may
still learn *ex post* that this is what it was. But at the moment all
we see is that the old party system, which has ossified over
seventy-five years, is crumbling, and that no stable new pattern

---

[2] "Effective number of parties" is an index that weighs parties by their vote
(or seat) shares. Specifically, it is measured by $1/v_i^2$, where v_i is the vote
share of party i. For example, if the vote shares of three parties are 0.5, 0.4,
and 0.1, the effective number is $1/0.42 = 2.38$.

has yet crystallized. Hence, this is a crisis: the old is dying and the new is not yet born. Moreover, if a realignment does ensue, it will include the rise of xenophobic parties that have little patience for democratic norms. As Piketty (2018) emphasizes, given multidimensional divisions of the electorate, different coalitions may emerge. Specifically, he speculates that in France and the US the most likely realignment is one of "globalists" against "nativists," while in Britain a "two-elite model" – wealthy against educated – is likely to persist. Note that this phenomenon is almost universal among developed democracies, so something strange is going on.

5.2 The Rise of Right-Wing Populism

The general mood is populist. Populism is an ideological twin of neo-liberalism. Both claim that social order is spontaneously created by a single demiurge: "the market" or "the people," the latter always in singular, as in "le peuple," "el pueblo," or "lud." Neither sees a role for institutions: spontaneity suffices. No wonder they appear together on the historical scene.

Many emergent parties portray themselves as "anti-system," "anti-establishment," or "anti-elite." They are "populist" insofar as the image of politics they project is one of an "elite" ("casta," cast, in the language of the Spanish Podemos; "swamp" in the language of Donald Trump) that betrays, abuses, or exploits undifferentiated "people" (Mudde 2004: 543). Such claims originate on the Left as well as the Right (Rooduijn and Akkerman 2017). Indeed, as the French 2017 elections show, they can also emerge from the center, even if ironically the parliament that resulted from this election is even more elitist in social terms than the outgoing one, just including fewer professional politicians. The populist parties are not anti-democratic in the sense that they do not advocate replacing elections by some other method of selecting governments. Even when they express a yearning for a strong leader, they want leaders to be elected. Political forces that question democracy do exist but they are completely marginal. In turn, these parties, again on the Left as well as on the Right, claim that the traditional representative institutions stifle the voice of "the people" and call for some new form of democracy that would better implement "popular sovereignty" (Pasquino 2008) and bring governments closer to "the people" (Canovan 2002). Popular initiative referendums are their favorite, but otherwise their projects for constitutional reforms are vague. Still, the populist image of politics is associated with the rejection of representative democracy and its replacement by a different, "direct" one. Hence, while the populist parties are not anti-democratic, they are anti-institutional in the sense of rejecting the traditional model of representative democracy. As a Mexican presidential candidate, Manuel López Obrador, exclaimed in the aftermath of his defeat in 2006, "to hell with your institutions" ("al diablo con vuestras instituciones").

On economic issues, left-wing parties are resolutely egalitarian. Those on the Right are more ambivalent: they want to retain the support of the traditional petite bourgeoisie, which wants lower taxes and a flexible labor market, while recruiting industrial workers, who want more job protection and more income redistribution (Iversflaten 2005). Both extremes are highly protectionist (Guiso et al. 2017, Rodrik 2017). Moreover, they oppose globalization and are strongly anti-Europe. The result is that at least in some countries, the economic policies of the radical Left and Right do not diverge by much. For example, comparing the electoral programs of the extreme Left candidate in the 2017 French presidential elections, Jean-Luc Mélenchon, and of Marine Le Pen, shows convergence on economic, social welfare, workers' rights, and protectionism issues.[3]

The similarities, however, end there. The sharp difference is with regard to immigration, immigrants, xenophobia, and racism. Some populist parties – Podemos in Spain, Syriza in Greece – are open to the coexistence of multiple cultures, view immigrants as net contributors to the economy, and take a strong stand against racism. In turn, the parties standardly referred to as "extreme" or "radical" Right are nationalist and xenophobic, or "nativist." They also tend to be racist and repressive. They adopt electoral strategies that emphasize the salience of "immigration" (Arzheimer 2013). Defending "national values" – a favorite phrase of Marine Le Pen – they advocate excluding immigrants from publicly provided social services, nationalistic indoctrination in education, banning Halal foods in school cafeterias, a dress code, etc. To this extent, they are authoritarian. With some unease, I follow Golder (2016) in using the label of "radical Right" to denote such parties.

While one may quibble about classifying particular parties, the trend is manifest. Figure 5.3 portrays the rise of radical Right parties in different sets of European and Anglo-Saxon democracies.[4] This picture, however, hides important differences among countries.

[3] See www.leparisien.fr/elections/presidentielle.
[4] Armingeon et al. (2016) use the label "populist right" and lump together what Golder (2016) would distinguish as "extreme" and "radical" Right.

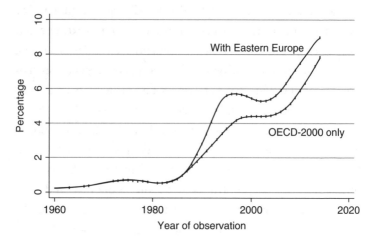

Figure 5.3. Average electoral support for radical Right, by year
Source: Armigeon et al. CDPS 2016, with modifications for
Hungary and Poland.Lowess smooth

The highest current share of radical Right parties are in
Switzerland, Austria, and Denmark, where they exceed 20 percent. In Austria and France, radical Right candidates won more
than 25 percent of votes in the first rounds of presidential elections. In turn, in five countries such parties either do not exist or
get no votes at the present. The trends are not homogeneous
either: radical Right parties gained strength only most recently in
Norway, Sweden, and Germany, while they peaked some time
ago in Belgium, Italy, and Japan. The open question is how to
treat the Republican Party in the United States. It now satisfies all
the criteria most scholars use to classify parties as radical Right,
even if Armingeon et al. (2016) do not classify it as such. More

They do not consider Fidesz in Hungary, Law and Justice (PiS) in Poland,
and UKIP as "Right," which I do. The data end in 2014.

90

generally, this classification does not take into account movements of traditional right-wing parties toward the extreme, which is perhaps why Armingeon et al. (2016) do not classify the Hungarian Fidesz and the Polish PiS as radical Right.

Table 5.1 *Share of votes of radical Right (countries that were members of the OECD as of 2000)*

Country	Maximal share[a]	Period	Last parliamentary	Last presidential[b]
Austria	28.2	2008–12	26.8	35.1
Belgium	14.0	2007–9	3.7	
Denmark	21.1	2015–	21.1	
Finland	19.1	2011–14	17.7	9.4
France	14.9	1997–2001	14.4[c]	26.0[c]
Germany	12.6	2017–	12.6	
Greece	14.4	2012–14	10.7[d]	
Iceland	3.0	2013–16	0.0	
Italy	25.8	1996–2000	4.1	
Japan	14.9	2012–13	2.1	
Luxembourg	2.3	1989–1999	0.0	
Netherlands	17.0	2002	13.1	
Norway	16.3	2013–17	15.2	
Spain	2.1	1979–81	0.0	
Sweden	12.9	2014–	12.9	
Switzerland	28.9	2007–10	26.6	
United Kingdom	3.1	2010–17	1.8	

Note: As of October 15, 2017. The radical Right has never won any votes in Australia, Canada, Ireland, New Zealand, or Portugal. (a) Maximal share of votes before the most recent parliamentary election, to the lower house if there is more than one. First-round results are reported for France. (b) Only where president is directly elected. (c) Front National + Debout La France. (d) Golden Dawn + ANEL.
Source: Armingeon et al. (2016), updated by own research.

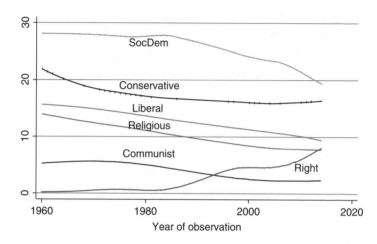

Figure 5.4. Vote shares of parties by years in countries that were members of the OECD before 2000
Lowess smooth. Data source: Armingeon et al. 2016 CDPS

Traditional parties lost electoral support among the potential voters, while the support for the radical Right has crept up. But is it because political opinions became more polarized, with voters moving to the extremes, or because traditional parties lost touch with their supporters? The crumbling of traditional parties need not entail an erosion of centrist, moderate preferences but just disgust with the parties themselves. When people believe that all professional politicians are the same, self-serving, dishonest, or corrupt, they turn against them whether they locate themselves on the left, right, or center. Hence, the erosion of traditional parties need not signify an erosion of the center.

The decline of traditional parties is manifest. In Figure 5.4 the parties are, from top to bottom, the leading social democratic, conservative, liberal, religious, and Communist

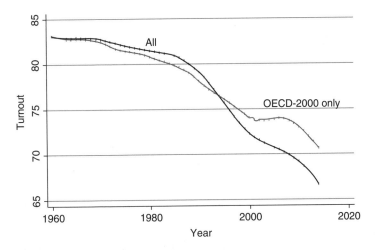

Figure 5.5. Turnout by year
Lowess smooth. Data source: Armingeon et al. 2016 CDPS

parties, as classified by Armingeon et al. (2016), while the lowest, rising, trend is for the parties of the radical Right. Perhaps surprisingly, this erosion of support for the traditional parties coincided with sharply declining turnouts (Figure 5.5).

This is not just a coincidence. Guiso et al. (2017) point out that if the decision to vote and the direction of the vote share are common determinants, one should expect the relation between turnout and right-wing vote to be negative. Within-country regressions of the vote shares of the radical Right on turnout in Figure 5.6 show that among the ten pre-2000 OECD members in which the radical Right exists, only in Denmark is the slope positive.[5]

---

[5] In the pooled data including all the countries, fixed-effects OLS regression generates the 95 percent confidence interval of the coefficient as [−0.168,

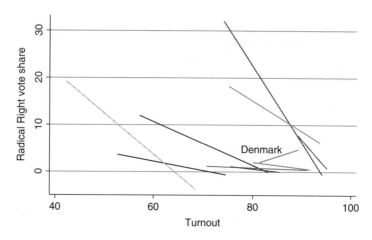

Figure 5.6. Turnout and radical Right vote share in ten developed democracies
Linear fit. Data source: Armingeon et al. 2016 CDPS

One cannot tell from the available data which part of the increase of electoral shares of the radical Right is due to an increase in the numbers of its supporters and which to the growing abstention of centrist voters. Yet it may well be that the increasing share of the radical Right is due more to the abstention of centrist voters than to an increase of extreme voters.

Why would centrist voters withdraw from the electoral process? There are two, not necessarily rival, hypotheses. One goes like this. The stagflation crisis of the 1970s, followed by the victories of Thatcher and Reagan, pushed traditional right-wing

−0.095; N = 1571]. Given that several countries do not have any radical Right parties, I also estimated a random effects Tobit regression, which gives an even more negative coefficient: [−0.487, −0.274; 453 uncensored observations].

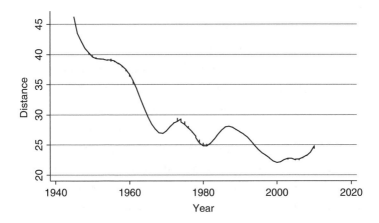

Figure 5.7. Ideological distance between center parties, by year
Data from the Manifestos Project, courtesy of Jose Maria
Maravall. The ideological scale ranges from −100 on the left to
+100 on the right. Countries include Western Europe plus
Australia, Israel, Japan, and New Zealand. Lowess smooth

parties to the right. For some reason, perhaps because of the
economic fiasco of the first year of Mitterrand's government, the
Social Democrats followed by also making a "virage" to
the right, embracing the language of "trade-offs" between equality and efficiency, fiscal discipline, and flexible labor markets.
As a result, the ideological distance between the two major
center-left and center-right parties has decreased sharply during
the post-war period, perhaps with a slight upturn following the
crisis of 2008, as shown in Figure 5.7.

Yet the convergence of party platforms on the left–right
dimension is not the only plausible explanation. Already Lipset
(1960) argued that political attitudes are two-dimensional, with

95

the second dimension being "authoritarianism."[6] According to Albright (2010: 714), the single left–right dimension "is steadily diminishing in its ability to summarize party behaviour." While economic issues still constitute the most important dimension along which parties compete in most countries (Huber and Inglehart 1995, Wagner 2012), social and cultural issues have gained in importance since the 1970s (Inglehart and Flanagan 1987). Moreover, it has been argued that in many countries the cultural and the economic dimensions do not neatly correlate with each other anymore, so that the political space cannot be characterized by a single left–right axis but has to be depicted as two-dimensional (Kitschelt 1994, Kriesi et al. 2006, 2012, Marks et al. 2006). Brady, Ferejohn, and Papano (2017), for example, find in a study of seven countries that traditional parties adopt more pro-immigration policies than their supporters and attribute the weakening of these parties to this distance: "immigration has driven a wedge between the major parties – those that regularly play a role in government – and their supporters and that this wedge opens up enormous space for new movements either inside existing parties or outside." For a long time, the rhetoric of the radical Right has been that "they are taking jobs from you," while recently it has become more along the lines of "you are paying for them," that the "middle class" is paying for the poor, particularly the immigrants, and particularly those with a different skin color. "Illegal immigrant households receive far more in federal welfare benefits than native American

---

[6] On general issues concerning bi-dimensionality and party strategies in the presence of a second dimension, see the special issue of *Party Politics* (2015, vol. 21(6)), with an introduction by Elias, Szocsik, and Zuber (2015).

households," Trump wrote in a 2016 Facebook post, "I will fix it." As Brady, Ferejohn, and Paparo (2017: 3) put it, "immigration puts a recognizable face on events that may well be properly attributable to other forces." Hence, the alternative story is that whatever the left–right distance among them, the traditional parties increased their distance from voter preferences on the immigration issue, thus alienating their supporters.

An open issue is why the center parties would remain distant from voters on the second dimension, whatever it is. A plausible explanation is provided by Dancygier (2017). Accommodating xenophobic preferences is costly for these parties in terms of votes because it causes people she refers to as "cosmopolitans" to move out of the electorate. Hence, center parties face a trade-off between winning the votes of some sectors of the potential electorate and losing them from other sectors. They adopt xenophobic postures when it is electorally advantageous and refrain from appealing to such attitudes when it would lead to the erosion of their traditional support. Even if they maximize their potential vote shares, in either case they face limits to how far they can move. Hence, in equilibrium, they still remain distant from some voters on the cultural dimension.

Before summarizing, it is instructive to look in more detail at a particular country, namely France. First, while a large majority, 71 percent, up from 57 percent in 2013, of French survey respondents now agree that "the notions of the Left and the Right are obsolete," 94 percent are still able to locate themselves on this dimension (Hastings 2018). So can 91 percent of Europeans (excluding Russia) in general (Cautres 2018). During the past forty years France experienced several partisan alternations in office, all governments focused on reducing unemployment, and yet unemployment never fell below 9 percent. Hence, as Teinturier (2018: 65) reports, voters ask themselves whether politics has any effect on their lives. Since 2013, between 75 and 83 percent of the French declared that "The democratic system functions rather badly in France. I have an impression that my ideas are not well represented." Moreover, about two-thirds agree that "Most politicians are corrupt" and between 83 and 89 percent that "They act principally in their personal interests." Politics evokes "disappointment" among 40 percent, "disgust" among 20 percent, "anger" among 13 percent, and "indifference" among 9 percent (all these numbers are from Teinturier 2018). Electoral abstention in legislative elections has increased sharply since the 1980s and in presidential elections since 2007. Together these patterns indicate that while the left–right dimension remains as salient as it was in the past, most people are just disgusted with the traditional parties.

At the same time, there is a general perception that the issue space is not unidimensional. Following Inglehart, Foucault (2018) sees the second dimension as broadly cultural, but without specifying its components or showing its independence of the economic dimension. In a daring novel (*Soumission*, 2015), Michel Houellebecq raises the specter of a confessional, Catholic-Islam coalition opposed to a secular, republican one. The only piece of hard evidence I could find is from Piketty (2018), who uses exit polls to classify voters according to their positive or negative attitudes toward redistribution and immigration, and shows that in 2017 they divided almost equally among the four cells of this two-by-two table. Hence, the evidence is that immigration divides people independently of the left–right dimension, but it is not clear what else does.

Finally, the result of the 2017 presidential election was a debacle for the traditional Left. Among their usual constituencies, the share of the Left vote among people between eighteen and thirty-nine years old fell from 31 percent in 2012 to 7 percent; among people with more than high-school education from 33 to 7 percent; among public employees from 41 to 8 percent. But it seems that most of the vote the Socialists lost was split between the extreme Left and the center, not benefiting the Right. In turn, while the 2017 election was the first one in which more workers voted for the extreme Right (Front National) than the Left, the largest party among them are non-voters (based on Foucault 2018).

In the end, even with all these data it is difficult to tell to what extent the recent political transformations in France are due to the general disaffection with the traditional parties – a crisis of representation – and to what extent they are due to an emerging salience of some second dimension that divides people independently from the economic one. Piketty (2018: 26–7) reports that the proportion of voters who say that there are "too many" immigrants in France has actually declined over time, as has the salience of the religious dimension. Hence, it is not clear whether the virtual disappearance of the traditional center-left and center-right parties is due to voters' disgust with politicians or to their distance from voters on the dimension of immigration.

More generally, we can see that support for traditional center parties has crumbled across Europe and that some centrist voters withdrew from the electorate, while the vote shares of radical Right parties, but not necessarily absolute numbers of their supporters, have increased. To what extent these transformations are due to a general rejection of parties and politicians and to what extent to the rise of some second, "cultural," dimension is difficult to weigh. Moreover, to repeat the caveat of Section 5.1, the rejection of party politics may be just a transitory phenomenon: new center parties may replace the traditional ones, mobilize centrist voters, and deter a further move of the electorate toward the radical Right, as at least for now seems to be happening in France. Yet it is also possible that the center will continue to erode and xenophobic, populist parties will continue to gain strength, or that the traditionally centrist parties will successfully prevent the electoral rise of the radical Right only by moving to that position themselves.

5.3 Decline of Support for Democracy in Surveys

All kinds of surveys are cited as evidence of declining support for democracy: "democratic backsliding" or "democratic deconsolidation." In particular Foa and Mounk (2016) find it alarming that in the six countries they examined, younger people find it less "essential to live in a democracy."[7] Armingeon and Guthman (2014) examined seventy-eight surveys in twenty-six European Union countries to compare support for democracy in 2007 and 2011. They found that this support fell in twenty countries and increased in six, with the total mean declining by 7.2 points. Countries that were most affected by the 2008 crisis,

---

[7] For a debate on Foa and Mounk, go to http://journalofdemocracy.org/online-exchange-%E2%80%9Cdemocratic-deconsolidation%E2%80%9D.

notably Greece and Spain, are where this support fell most. Similar results about the effect of the 2008 crisis emerge from surveys conducted by the World Values Studies that ask people whether they have confidence in democracy, experts, the army, or strong leaders, albeit with more heterogeneous patterns over the longer run, and with the United States showing the sharpest decline in the relative standing of democracy since the 1994–8 period (Weakliem 2016a). Surveys also show declining confidence in other, not just representative, institutions. At least in the United States, confidence also declined sharply for newspapers, television, banks, big business, religion, schools, and the medical system (Weakliem 2016b, based on data from Gallup).

Are these numbers signs of a crisis of democracy? If a crisis is defined by these numbers, then this is just a tautology, albeit one that is frequently made by those who produce them. But should we take them as harbingers of a collapse of democracy? Titles of popular articles in which these numbers "ring bells for democracy" are ubiquitous. Yet while such numbers are disheartening, there is not a shred of evidence that they predict anything. Six months before the coup in Chile only 27.5 percent of respondents thought that "a military coup is convenient for Chile" (Navia and Osorio 2018). Whether democracy requires democrats, whether its continued existence depends on individual attitudes, is a controversial issue. Even if it does, the causal relation between answers to survey questions and the erosion of democracy must depend on the actions of organized political groups.

Responses to survey questions are informative but not predictive. For one, no one knows what people in different countries and at different times understand by "democracy" when they are asked whether "democracy" is the best form of government or whether it is essential that their country be governed "democratically." While elites see democracy in institutional terms, several surveys indicate that mass publics often conceive of it in terms of "social and economic equality." Moreover, even if recent surveys indicate that many people would want to be governed by "strong leaders" and many others by non-partisan "experts," does it mean that they do not want to have a voice in choosing the leaders or the experts? The taste for selecting governments through elections is an acquired one, but it is addictive once acquired. Wanting governments to be effective, hoping that they will be competent and effective in improving people's lives, does not imply abdication from the right to choose them and to replace them when they fail. Finally, with all the variations in the support for democracy shown by surveys conducted in different developed countries over the past thirty-five years, democracy collapsed in none of them. We may be worried when few people declare confidence in political parties, parliaments, or governments, when the belief that democracy is the best system of government declines among the mass public, or when the yearning for strong leaders or the rule by experts increases. But the predictive power of answers to such questions for the outright collapse of democracy is null. One should not draw inferences about the survival of democracy from answers to survey questions.

6

Potential Causes

Here's an Irish joke. A couple of tourists gets lost while trekking in Ireland. They ask a peasant cultivating his field, "How do we get from here to Dublin?" He responds, "First, you do not begin from here." Where to begin the explanations? Globalization, technological change, breakdown of class compromise, immigration, authorization of prejudices by some insurgent politicians, or something still else? The purpose of this chapter is just to catalogue the potential explanations, without attempting to adjudicate among them. Issues entailed in identifying causality are raised in Chapter 7.

6.1 The Economy: Income Stagnation, Inequality, and Mobility

The instinct is to start with the economy, and this is where I begin. The economic developments of the past decades can be grossly characterized by three transformations that generated two effects. These transformations are: (1) decline of growth rates of the already developed countries; (2) increase in income inequality among individuals and households, as well as a declining labor share in manufacturing; and (3) decline of employment in industry and the rise of the service sector, particularly of low-paying service jobs. Here is some evidence.

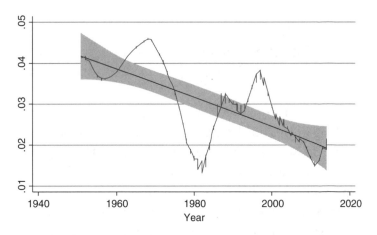

Figure 6.1. Rate of growth of per capita income by year of
countries that were members of the OECD before 2000
The irregular line is a lowess smooth, the fitted line fractional
polynomial regression with 95% confidence interval

The rates of growth of developed democracies, which
I take as countries that were members of the OECD before
2000, declined from about 4 percent in the aftermath of
World War II to about 2 percent currently. Figure 6.1 shows
the annual averages and the trend. As shown in Figure 6.2, the
average within-country inequality increased sharply (the picture looks almost identical for countries that were members of
the OECD before 2000). Figure 6.3 shows that the average
labor share took a precipitous dip from about 1980. In turn, as
shown in Figure 6.4, the average employment in industry
declined over time in absolute terms in the developed democracies, while employment in services increased.

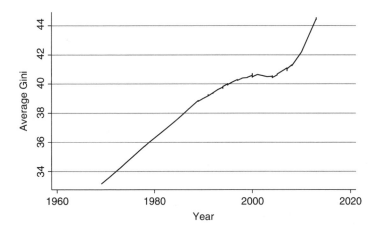

Figure 6.2. Average Gini coefficient of pre-fisc incomes in Europe,
Japan, Australia, New Zealand, by year
Data source: Armingeon et al. 2016 CDPS. Lowess smooth

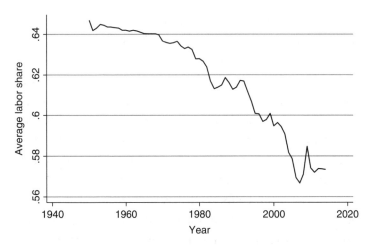

Figure 6.3. Average labor share by year among countries that were
members of the OECD before 2000

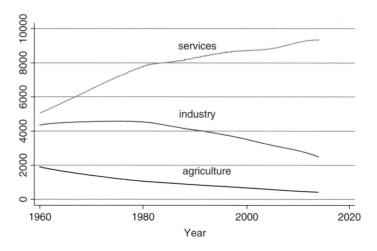

Figure 6.4. Average employment by sector over time, absolute numbers
Lowess smooth. Source: Armingeon et al. 2016 CPDS

The first effect of the combination of declining growth rates with increasing inequality is the stagnation of lower incomes, which has been exceptionally long-lasting in the United States, portrayed in Figure 6.5. The picture is somewhat different in the remaining OECD-2000 countries. Figure 6.6 shows that while the distance between the income of the top and bottom 10 percent of recipients increased sharply from the 1980s onwards, incomes below the median continued to creep up until all incomes were hit by the crisis of 2008.

The second effect is the erosion of the belief in material progress. According to the Pew Research Center (Spring 2015 Global Attitudes Survey), 60 percent of respondents in the United States and 64 percent in Europe now believe that their children will be worse off financially than they are.

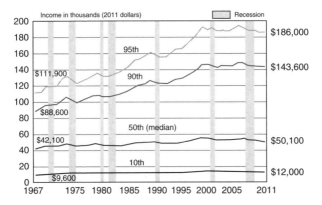

Figure 6.5. Real household income at selected
percentiles, 1967 to 2011
Source: United States Census Bureau, public
domain.

Moreover, these are not just perceptions. Chetty et al. (2016)
calculate that in the United States 90 percent of thirty-year-
old offspring were better off than their parents at the same age
in 1970, while in 2010 only 50 percent were. This collapse of
the deeply ingrained belief in intergenerational progress is
a phenomenon at a civilizational scale. The expectation of
material progress has been an essential ingredient for Western
civilization during the past 200 years. Since about 1820 every
generation in Europe and the United States lived and
expected to live better than their parents, and yet this belief
is being shattered. This is certainly a transformation that can
have profound cultural and political consequences.

Why did these economic transformations occur? Two
hypotheses are straightforward and plausible. One is "globalization," the combination of the liberalization of commodity

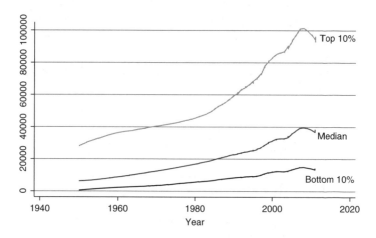

Figure 6.6. Average incomes of selected groups, OECD-2000
countries excluding the United States
Calculated from PWT9.0 and WIDER, in 2011 PPP USD Lowess
smooth

and capital markets, combined with the Chinese reforms.
The second is an *autogolpe* (self-coup) of the bourgeoisie,
the breakdown of class compromise. Both of these events
have a definite date, more or less 1978–80, so they cannot be
distinguished by rough timing. They may or may not be
associated but I discuss them separately.

The effect of China is a subject of much controversy.
Autor et al. (2013; see also Acemoglu et al. 2016) conclude that
rising imports cause higher unemployment, lower labor-force
participation, and reduced wages in local labor markets that
house import-competing industries. They attribute one-
quarter of the contemporaneous aggregate decline in United
States manufacturing employment to import competition from
China. Yet Rothwell (2017) questions the Autor et al. estimates,

concluding that foreign competition does not appear to elevate the risk of job loss to a greater extent than domestic competition, and that people living in the communities most exposed to foreign competition are no worse off on average. Rothwell and Diego-Rosell (2016) conclude that "Surprisingly, there appears to be no link whatsoever between greater exposure to trade competition or competition from immigrant workers and support for nationalist policies in America, as embodied by the Trump campaign." In turn, Miao (2016) points out that import competition lowers prices, and identifies a significant welfare gain from trade with China. Moreover, in a recent review of the literature, Helpman (2016) concludes that increased wage inequality is due mainly to factors other than commodity trade. Hence, economists need to sort out their disagreements. What is clear is that some people lost as a result of globalization and were not compensated by redistributive or other policies (Rodrik 2017).

An alternative explanation is the breakdown of class compromise. The most startling picture is for the United States, portrayed in Figure 6.7. The same is true for some, albeit not all, other advanced economies after 1999, shown in Figure 6.8. Other sources show the same to have occurred in Germany as of 1997, Japan as of 2002, and the UK as of 1988.

Until about 1978, increases in wages almost exactly followed increases in productivity, so that the functional distribution of income was stable. Industrial workers were organized by unions protected by the state and, with almost

109

Figure 6.7. Disconnect between productivity and a typical worker's compensation, 1948–2014
Source: Economic Policy Institute.

full employment, unions had monopoly power over labor markets. Anticipating that excessive wage demands would cause firms to invest less, wherever they were sufficiently centralized, unions exercised wage restraint. Government policies were subject to the same constraint as unions, namely that excessive income taxation would reduce investment, and thus future consumption. In turn, facing moderate wage and taxation demands, firms not only invested but could also live with unions and with democracy. As a result, a "democratic class compromise" naturally emerged. Governments managed this compromise by regulating markets, providing social services, and offering incentives for investment and innovation.

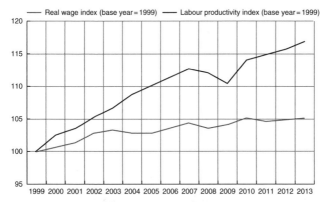

Note: Labour productivity is defined as GDP per employed person and used GDP in constant 2005 PPP$ for all countries. G20 advanced economies include: Australia, Canada, France, Germany, Italy, Japan, the Republic of Korea, the United Kingdom and the United States. Both indices are based on a weighted average of all the countries in the group that takes into account labour productivity and the size of paid employment.

Figure 6.8. Productivity and wage index (G20 advanced economies)
Source: ILO.

This compromise was shattered in the United Kingdom and the United States by the respective victories of Thatcher and Reagan, whose first targets were the unions,[1] and eroded more gradually in most other countries. As a consequence, as shown in Figure 6.9, the average union density dropped by more than ten percentage points between the peak in 1980 and 2010. Perhaps the most consequential policy of the Thatcher government was the stealth opening of capital account, which changed the trade-offs between

---

[1] "Unions" was the most frequently used word both in the 1979 Conservative Manifesto and in Thatcher's electoral campaign. Under the combined pressure of unemployment and of hostile legislation, the trade union movement was seriously weakened, losing 17 percent of its membership in five years.

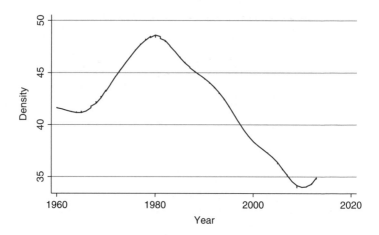

Figure 6.9. Union density by year in countries that were members of the OECD before 2000
Lowess smooth. Source: Armigenon et al. 2016 CPDS

redistribution and growth and thus forced both major political parties to reduce the extent of the redistribution they proposed (Dunn 2000). The opening of capital account was not an issue in the election of 1979 when Mrs. Thatcher came to office. Yet once the decision was made, the entire spectrum of feasible policies was moved. It bears emphasis that this offensive by the Right was premeditated, planned, vigorously promoted by all kinds of think tanks, and coercively spread by the influence of the United States in the international financial institutions, codified as the "Washington Consensus."

Whatever the causes, plus automation, these processes generated winners and losers. For future reference, it makes sense to distinguish: (1) actual losers, those who lost stable jobs with living wages in industry and either moved to lower-paid services or were forced to retire or became long-term unemployed; (2) prospective losers, those who fear this fate; (3) non-winners, principally the self-employed, the traditional petite bourgeoisie whose material conditions did not change much one way or another; and (4) winners, the recipients of profit incomes, however disguised.

6.2 Divisiveness: Polarization, Racism, and Hostility

When thinking about the intensity of political divisions, we need to consider two distinct aspects. (1) Distributions of preferences over some general policy dimension (liberal–conservative in the United States, left–right in Europe) or over specific issues, such as immigration. These distributions can be characterized in terms of "polarization": a population is polarized if individual preferences divide people into clusters that are internally homogeneous and distant from each other (Esteban and Ray 1994). (2) The actions that people with particular preferences are or are not willing to engage in with regard to members of other group(s). This is important because people with the same ideological profile may have different postures toward those with whom they disagree and may be willing or not to engage in hostile acts against them.

The ideological distance of party supporters in the United States, portrayed in Figure 6.10, has sharply increased in the past twenty-three years. Whether the same is true across the European countries is more difficult to diagnose because of the prevalence of multi-party systems, in which people sort themselves out around parties occupying several

Distribution of Democrats and Republicans on a 10-item scale of political values

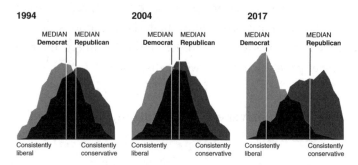

Notes: Ideological consistency based on a scale of 10 political values questions (see methodology). The light grey area in this chart represents the ideological distribution of Democrats and Democratic-leaning independents; the dark grey area of Republicans and Republican-leaning independents. The overlap of these two distributions is shaded black.

Figure 6.10. Democrats and Republicans more ideologically divided than in the past
Source: Pew Research Center, public domain (see www .pewresearch.org/terms-and-conditions).

positions of the left–right spectrum. Given the availability of several parties, one would expect that supporters of each are more homogeneous, but the overall distance between them is more difficult to characterize. Indeed, the evidence that voters moved away from the center is ambiguous outside the United States. The distribution of individual positions on the left–right dimension, studied by Medina (2015: figure 1) in eighteen European countries, tends to be trimodal, with a large mode at the center and small modes left and right of center. Between 2002–3 and 2008, the mean position shifted to the left in six countries, to the right in six, and in six it remained statistically indistinguishable. In terms of polarization, the size of the center mode decreased in seven countries

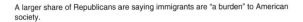

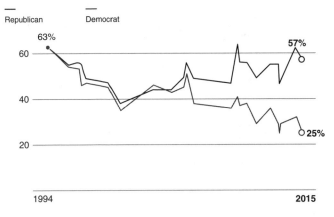

Figure 6.11. Immigration wasn't always a partisan issue
Source: Pew Research Center, public domain (see www
.pewresearch.org/terms-and-conditions).

(Belgium, Czech Republic, Denmark, Finland, Germany, Poland, and Slovenia), increased in three, and remained the same in eight. In turn, Moral and Best (2018) found that the polarization of citizens increased in Australia, Denmark, Sweden, and the United States, but decreased in Germany and the Netherlands. Hence, even if in some countries people moved away from the center, there is no general European trend.

As shown in Figure 6.11, the increase of polarization is particularly evident with regard to immigration. Immigration, in some countries specifically the inflow of refugees, is also the most salient and divisive issue in Europe. The distribution of

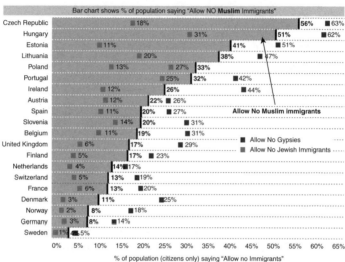

Figure 6.12. European attitudes to immigrants: racial differences
Source: European Social Survey.

postures toward immigration is clearly bimodal across Europe (Spoon and Kluwer 2015). Moreover, while attitudes toward immigration vary across European countries, it is striking that survey respondents distinguish the potential immigrants by ethnicity or race: as shown in Figure 6.12, Gypsies are less desirable in almost all countries than Muslims, who are in turn less desirable than Jews.

The language of "immigration" used by the Right amalgamates two distinct issues. One is control over the current flow of foreigners across borders, which is the standard-bearer of the language of "national sovereignty." But note that the current net flow between the United States and

Mexico is southward: according to Pew Research Center (2015), between 2008 and 2014 the Mexican population in the United States fell by 140,000. Hence, if President Trump does build a wall, it will keep more Mexicans in than it prevents from coming. Indeed, there are reasons to think that if this border was completely open, there would be fewer undocumented Mexicans in the United States at any time: lowering the risk of not being able to come back would reduce the incentives to stay illegally. The same does not hold for countries exposed to a massive inflow of refugees, but it does hold for France, where the net inflow is relatively low. In fact, when Mme. Le Pen or President Trump refer to "immigrants," they mean the third-generation offspring of immigrants, who happen to have a different physiognomy. Both invoke a myth of a "national culture," some traditional way of life, that is being undermined by the presence of "immigrants." "Immigrants" is just a code word for racism.

As sacrilegious as it may seem, it is useful to delve into the conceptual relation between racism and multiculturalism. The obvious difference is that racism claims inequality between groups, treating them as innately superior and inferior. The second difference is that the races are defined by the racists, and in their view one is a member of a race by virtue of origin, independently of one's choice, while the ideology of multiculturalism allows individuals to choose their cultural identity. Yet the identities we choose for ourselves are not always those in terms of which we are perceived by others. In a beautiful phrase of Amitav Gosh, we leave "shadow lines": I may not see myself as Jewish or Muslim, yet others may still see me as one. What these ideologies have in common is the ontology of social fragmentation that should be acknowledged by society and the state. As Michaels (2007: 3) observed, "the goal of overcoming racism, which had sometimes been identified as the goal of creating a 'color-blind' society, was now reconceived as the goal of creating a diverse, that is, a color-conscious, society." Their commonality becomes clear when juxtaposed against the ideology of "republicanism": the idea that as citizens we are anonymous, that when people with different features and different self-identifications enter the public sphere they lose all their qualities and must be treated equally because they are indistinguishable (Rosanvallon 2004). In spite of all their differences, racism and multiculturalism are both ideologies that fraction society into distinct groups.

When combined with cultural relativism, postmodern ideology implies a multiplicity of truths. The truth of a statement is authenticated by the identity of the speaker and all identities are equally authoritative. It creates a world that allows for differences but precludes disagreements (Michaels 2007). If I say "As a pink male, I believe the news is . . ., " one can claim that this news is false for him or her. But you cannot persuade me and I cannot persuade you: each of us has our own truth. There is nothing to talk about: a recent study reports that in 2017 a Thanksgiving dinner with guests from electoral districts dominated by different parties lasted 30–50 minutes less than with exclusively co-partisans (the average was 257 minutes; Chen and Rohla 2018). Our beliefs have no authority over others because they are conditioned by our identity. In a relativist world, the news of others are all "fake" and there is no procedure by which they could be determined to be true or false: this is a "post-truth" world.

In an exceptionally well-informed and incisive analysis, Lewandowsky, Ecker, and Cook (2017) report some results of research:

1. "Corrections are rarely fully effective: that is, despite being corrected, and despite acknowledging the correction, people by and large continue to rely at least partially on information they know to be false ... In some circumstances, when the correction challenges people's worldviews, belief in false information may ironically even increase" (p. 355).
2. Falsehoods induce some people to conclude that truth is unknowable even when the false message is not credible.
3. Propagating falsehoods diverts people from recognizing other messages as true.
4. People tend to persist with beliefs they admit to be false if they believe they are shared by others.

They conclude, "We are now facing a situation in which a large share of the populace is living in an epistemic space that has abandoned conventional criteria of evidence, internal consistency, and fact-seeking ... An obvious hallmark of a post-truth world is that it empowers people to choose their own reality, where facts and objective evidence are trumped by existing beliefs and prejudices" (pp. 361–2). What distinguishes people is not information but alternative epistemologies. Powerful evidence presented by Meeuwis et al. (2018) shows that investors who had different models of the economy modified their portfolios differently in response to the US election of 2016, and the differences ran along party lines.

THE PRESENT: WHAT IS HAPPENING?

Moreover, even when the views of particular individuals remain fixed, their attitudes toward those with whom they disagree can be less or more hostile. In the United States, 86 percent of Democrats and 91 percent of Republicans have unfavorable views of the other party, with 41 percent of Democrats and 45 percent of Republicans seeing the other party as a "threat to the nation" (Acherbach and Clement 2016). Poignant anecdotes about experiences of discrimination and abuse in everyday life abound, and many systematic data indicate that the general level of anger and hostility is on the rise. In 2012, 33 percent of Democrats and 43 percent of Republicans described themselves as angry at the opposing party's presidential candidate "most of the time" or "just about always," while by 2016 the percentage of Democratic voters who said they were this angry at Trump rose to 73 percent, and the percentage of Republicans with that level of hostility toward Hillary Clinton increased to 66 percent. Where we have more systematic evidence, albeit only for the most recent years, is with regard to "hate crimes." In the United States their incidence in the nine major metropolitan areas increased 23.3 percent from 2015 to 2016, with a total of 13,037 (NBC 2017). Another source reports that they jumped in the aftermath of the election, with over 1,000 incidents self-reported between November 9 and December 12, 2016 (SPLC 2016). Overall, anti-immigrant incidents (315) remain the most reported, followed by anti-black (221), anti-Muslim (112), and anti-LGBT (109). Anti-Trump incidents numbered twenty-six. Britain saw an increase of over 40 percent in self-reported hate crime incidents between

2015 and 2016. In addition to race-based hate crimes, Britain also saw a rise in hate crimes based on sexual orientation. Galop, a London-based LGBT anti-violence charity, reported that hate crimes motivated by sexual orientation rose 147 percent during the late summer of 2016. Other countries across Europe have also experienced an increased rate of hate crimes over the past several years. Between 2014 and 2015, Germany reported a 77 percent increase in hate crimes. Amnesty International reported that incidents of race-based violence are at an all-time high since World War II in Germany. Statistics collected by Germany's Interior Ministry show that asylum shelters were attacked 1,031 times in 2015, a drastic increase from 199 attacks in 2014 and sixty-nine attacks in 2013. In Spain, the Spanish Federation of Islamic Religious Entities reported that anti-Islam attacks increased from forty-eight in 2014 to 534 in 2015. Additionally, Spain's Interior Ministry published statistics for 2015 reporting hundreds of hate crimes based on disability, ideology, and sexual orientation (Human Rights Brief 2017). France seems to be the exception, with racist crimes (anti-Semitic, anti-Muslim, anti-Roma) having peaked in 2015 and then falling 44.7 percent, from 2,034 to 1,125, between 2015 and 2016 (Franceinfo 2017).

These, albeit unsystematic, facts show that the divisions that rip several countries apart are not merely political but have deep roots in society. These two levels are obviously related but which way the causality runs is hard to determine, as social and political polarization may feed on one another (Moral and Best 2018). What these facts do tell us is that we should not overpoliticize our understanding of the current situation – that we should not reduce it to the actions of politicians. The incessant complaints about Trump's temper and incompetence should not obscure that fact that his election and his continuing support reflect something deeper, something that lurks in the everyday life of society.

7

Where to Seek Explanations?

7.1 Methodological Issues

As we have already seen, explanations can begin with the economy, culture, or strategies of traditional parties; perhaps all of them, perhaps some combinations. Yet most of the pictures shown in previous chapters represent averages for groups of countries over time – central tendencies – while particular countries are far from being the same. As of 2014, there were no radical Right parties in Australia, Canada, Ireland, Luxembourg, New Zealand, Portugal, or Spain. The income shares of the top 1 percent of recipients show a sharp increase from the 1970s in the Anglo-Saxon countries, while they remained stable in Germany, Japan, France, Sweden, Denmark, and the Netherlands. The proportion of survey respondents saying that immigration should be decreased ranges from 25 percent in Australia, through 40 percent in the United States, to 69 percent in the United Kingdom (Gallup surveys in 2012 and 2014). Strikingly, Figure 7.1 shows that even Germany and France clearly differ in the relation between wage growth and productivity growth.

It bears emphasis that the US is in many ways an outlier. It is the only economically developed democracy where a candidate with a radical Right program has won an election. While a decline of median incomes occurred in most

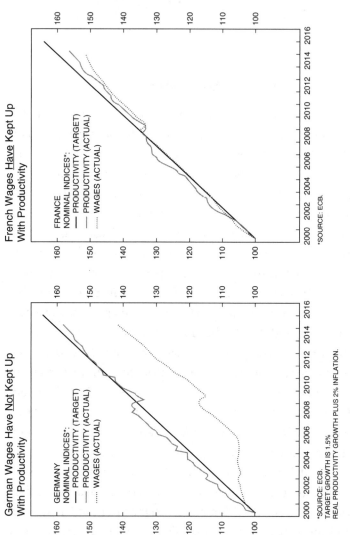

Figure 7.1. Wages and productivity in Germany and France
Source: European Central Bank.

countries only after 2008, in the United States they have stagnated over a longer period. Top incomes rose more in the United States than in other countries. Political polarization is exceptionally sharp. It is a country experiencing a diminishing international influence, as well as deteriorating infrastructure, education, and health. Perhaps most symptomatic are the recent data generated by Case and Deaton (2017) concerning mortality patterns of white males aged 45–54, which show that these mortality rates declined sharply in France, Germany, the United Kingdom, Australia, and Sweden, while they have increased since the late 1990s in the United States. Finally, it is the only presidential system with indirect elections, generating issues of legitimacy when a candidate who does not obtain a majority of votes is declared as the winner according to constitutional norms.

As these cross-country differences evidence, what we have seen thus far is only the zeitgeist, the spirit of the time. But the devil is in the details. How then to identify causal relations? Global causes are not sufficient: globalization cannot explain the differences between Germany and France. At least some interaction between global causes and national factors is necessary. I am skeptical that standard social science methods will take us far. There are many common trends and time series are relatively short, so I am concerned that we would find causality where there is none. Indeed, while studies at the aggregate level tend to find relations between economic variables and support for the radical Right, individual-level data leave a lot of doubt (Kates and Tucker 2017: 1–2). Moreover, when different states of the world co-evolve over time, it is hard to determine which way the causality runs (Dancygier and Laitin 2014). Finally, cross-country observations are not independent: there is diffusion as well as dissuasion, with debates as to whether Trump's victory increased support for the Front National or whether it dissuaded Dutch voters from voting for Geert Wilders in 2017.

It is not obvious how to proceed, but it is instructive to look at the micro level.

7.2 Voting for and Supporting the Radical Right

The obvious temptation is to rationalize these attitudes in economic terms, as competition for employment, defense of wages from competition, etc. Is support for the radical Right related to individual or collective economic conditions, such as income, experiencing economic difficulties, having suffered a job loss, fearing a job loss, and the like? A stronger version of this question is whether these postures are economically rational, that is, whether policies offered by the radical Right are in the best interest of those who support it. One cannot assume, however, that individuals accurately perceive the economic conditions or understand the consequences of particular policies. Even perceptions of one's own economic situation are tainted by partisan loyalties or other biases. One striking example is that following the election of Donald Trump, Democratic supporters revised downward the perceptions of their own economic situation over the past five years while Republican supporters revised it upwards (Brady, Ferejohn, and Paparo 2017). Perceptions of general economic conditions are even more vulnerable to such biases (Stokes 2001, Maravall and Przeworski 2001). Hence, it is a different question whether people rationalize their political postures in economic terms or whether they are rational in the sense of being based on accurate beliefs about the world.

The strongest support in favor of the effects of actual job losses in the United States is provided by Autor et al. (2017), who found a robust positive effect of rising import competition on Republican vote share gains and attributed Trump's victory directly to imports from China. In turn, in a massive study of regions within fifteen Western European countries between 1988 and 2007, Colantone and Stanig (2017: 1) report that "At the district level, a stronger import shock leads to: (1) an increase in support for nationalist parties; (2) a general shift to the right in the electorate; and (3) an increase in support for radical right parties. These results are confirmed by the analysis of individual-level vote choices. In addition, we find evidence that voters respond to the shock in a sociotropic way." Nevertheless, the effect of job loss on the vote for the radical Right is small: the difference between regions in the 75th percentile of job loss and those in the 25th percentile is 0.7 points of the vote share. In another study of several countries, Guiso et al. (2017) learn that experiencing current income difficulties makes people less inclined to vote, but if they do vote they are more inclined to vote for the "populist" parties, while the experience of having lost a job during the past five years reduces the probability of voting without having an effect on the direction of the vote. Yet Margalit (2013), as well as Ayta, Rau, and Stokes (2017), find that the political effects of unemployment are conditional on the general economic situation and wane with time. The most detailed study of the 2016 election in the United States that I found concludes that

> The results show mixed evidence that economic distress
> has motivated Trump support. His supporters are less
> educated and more likely to work in blue collar
> occupations, but they earn relatively high household
> incomes and are no less likely to be unemployed or
> exposed to competition through trade or immigration.
> On the other hand, living in racially isolated communities
> with worse health outcomes, lower social mobility, less
> social capital, greater reliance on social security income
> and less reliance on capital income, predicts higher levels
> of Trump support. (Rothwell and Diego-Rosell 2016)

There is also evidence that fear, rather than actual experience,
drives radical Right postures. Minkenberg (2000: 187) finds
right-wing supporters among the "second-to-last fifth of postmodern society, a stratum which is rather secure but objec-
tively can still lose something." Kates and Tucker (2017: 3)
conclude that "only pessimism about one's own financial
future is positively correlated with far right ideological iden-
tification." Fossati (2014) learns that individuals in occupations that have a high unemployment rate are more likely to
vote on the basis of economic considerations.

Particularly puzzling are the results of Andrews, Jilke,
and Van de Walle (2014), who used a survey conducted across
Europe in 2010 concerning perceptions of social tensions
along four dimensions: the poor and the rich, managers and
workers, old and young people, and different racial and ethnic
groups. What I find perplexing is that people who experience
income difficulties are more likely to perceive higher tensions
on all four dimensions. One would think that some would
find the culprit for their conditions among the rich, others

among the management, still others in the disproportionate income of old people, and some would blame immigrants. Yet people who perceive high tension on one dimension also perceive it on all the other dimensions. Neither class nor racist ideology has a clear sway on the way people analyze their conditions. They blame everyone because they do not know whom to blame.

In light of this, context matters. Ivarsflaten (2008) shows that radical Right parties are successful only if they appeal on the immigration issues, regardless of economic changes or political corruption. The conclusions she draws, however, are flawed because she does not consider why some anti-establishment parties use this issue while others do not. Dancygier (2010), in turn, argues that support for the radical Right is larger when poor economic conditions are combined with high immigration and when the immigrants have electoral power, so that incumbents have incentives to extend material benefits to immigrants.

Yet not everyone agrees about the relevance of economic factors. Inglehart and Norris (2016) find support for populist parties among people who report income difficulties and have experienced unemployment, but they conclude – I am not clear on what basis – that "cultural backlash" is a more convincing explanation. Hainmueller and Hopkins (2014: 227) question the relevance of economic factors for anti-immigration postures. "Overall," they report, "hypotheses grounded in self-interest have fared poorly, meaning that there is little accumulated evidence that citizens primarily form attitudes about immigration based on its effects on their personal economic situation." Instead, they claim, these attitudes are driven by "sociotropic concerns about its cultural impacts." I have no idea what this means, other than racism. Indeed, Lee and Roemer (2006) calculated that racism, specifically opposing the welfare services because they would also include people with different skin color, is economically costly to poor whites in the United States.

While the evidence that natives react negatively to people who differ from them is abundant, the origins of such postures remain obscure. If they do not reflect economic conditions, where do such postures come from? What makes people adopt xenophobic, often unabashedly racist, postures? What makes them willing to engage in hostile acts with regard to people who look different, speak a different language, or eat different foods? The psychological explanations favored by Hainmueller and Hopkins (2014) just relabel what we observe in a "scientific" language without providing enlightenment.

In turn, there is evidence that attitudes change as a function of other transformations. McCarty, Poole, and Rosenthal (2016) demonstrate a very strong relationship between income inequality and polarization in the United States House of Representatives from 1947 on. Another piece of evidence is that the perception of immigration as an important policy issue followed the increase of net immigration into the United Kingdom (IPSOS/MORI 2013). Still, a rival explanation is that xenophobia, racism, nativism, bigotry, and other prejudices were always present – German immigrants into the United States were "Krauts," Italians "Dagos," Japanese "Japs," Poles "Polacks," and they were only temporarily suppressed by hypocrisy, which suddenly lost its "civilizing force" (Elster 1998) because some politicians made them public. One startling piece of evidence is a survey conducted in the United States in 1939: the respondents were asked whether the country should receive 10,000 German, mainly Jewish, children, with 61 percent saying "No." Some Germans and Japanese continued to be nationalistic even after the atrocities committed by these countries during the war, and the language of "patriotism," recently evoked by right-wing parties, just authorized these attitudes to enter the public sphere. Perhaps Trump just liberated every preexisting prejudice from the censorship of political correctness.

All of this is second hand. I suggest a magisterial review of this literature by Golder (2016), who advocates combining contextual conditions and individual characteristics. It may be, however, easier said than done. From what we know as of now, it seems that the actual losers from globalization tend to vote Right and that the prospect of job loss frightens the potential losers. Yet while all these effects are statistically significant, they explain only a small part of radical Right postures. The origins of these postures remain opaque.

This is a paltry conclusion and it may disappoint many readers. But one should not believe the flood of accounts that have all the answers. If you read papers by economists, you will find that the political postures are explained by economic situations; if you read papers by psychologists the secret will lie in some psychological traits. I find neither explanation convincing: regression analyses of political postures on economic conditions always find some conditions that are statistically significant but explain very little; psychologists tend to relabel what they seek to explain and claim the relabeled feature is the cause. Our intellectual deformation is to always find some sense in complex situations, to suppose that diverse phenomena that surprise us must be somehow related, that everything must have a cause. I have listed various factors and briefly summarized each of several recent transformations – economic, cultural, and purely political – that may have engendered the current political situation, which is no more than a catalogue, and the conclusion is paltry because it says that we cannot tell whether they are related and which matters most. But that is the best, I believe, we can do given what we now know.

8

What May Be Unprecedented?

Before we can begin thinking about the future, it is useful to place the current situation in the context of what we have learned about the past. To the extent that some aspects of present conditions repeat those of the past, we can draw on the lessons of history suggested by the comparisons of consolidated democracies that collapsed and of those that survived earlier in time. Yet history does not illuminate the future when the present conditions are unprecedented, so there is nothing to draw lessons from. This is why we need to place the present in the context of the past.

A simple statistical analysis indicates that, even ignoring the fact that democracy in the US is 200 years old, given the current income of the United States, the probability that the incumbent would not hold an election or hold one making it impossible for the opposition to win is 1 in 1.8 million country years. If one believes in drawing lessons from history, an outright collapse of democracy in a country with the per capita income of the United States today is out of the realm of the imaginable. In spite of frequent references to these tragic events, looking back at the advent of fascism in Europe in the 1920s and 1930s is not instructive for the simple reason that the countries where fascism came to power were miserably poor compared to now. The per capita income (in 1996 Geary–Khamis PPP USD, from Maddison 2011) of Italy in 1922 was $2,631 while as of 2008 it was $19,909; of Germany it was \$3,362 in 1932 and \$20,801 in 2008; of Austria \$2,940 in 1932 and \$24,131 in 2008. This was just a different world.

It was also a different world ideologically. The extreme parties during the interwar period were anti-democratic (Capoccia 2005): both Communists and fascists openly sought to replace a system based on individual representation through elections. Communists derided democracy as a mask over the "dictatorship of the bourgeoisie" (Lenin 1919) and fought to replace it by a "dictatorship of the proletariat" led by a single party. Fascists disdained democracy as a system that promotes artificial conflicts between classes and strived to replace it with a system based on negotiated compromises among corporations organized along functional bases (Cassese 2011). Both offered a promise to replace "politics" with "rational administration." Both had a broad appeal, not only in Europe but around the world, from Argentina to Mongolia. Yet both these ideologies are now dead and buried. The "anti-system" parties of today are not anti-democratic. While the label of "fascist" is carelessly brandished to stigmatize these political forces, these parties do not advocate replacing elections by some other way of selecting rulers. They are ugly – most people view racism and xenophobia as ugly – but these parties campaign under the slogan of return-ing to "the people" the power usurped by elites, which they see as strengthening democracy. In the words of a Trump advertise-ment, "Our movement is about replacing a failed and corrupt political establishment with a new government controlled by you, the American people."[1] Marine Le Pen promised to call for a referendum on Europe, in which "you, the people, will decide."

---

[1] See www.youtube.com/watch?v=vST61W4bGm8.

Table 8.1 *Economic conditions in democracies that fell or did not fall before 2008 and the post-2008 means for democracies that survived*

	Fell	Didn't fall	Now	
	Mean	Mean	N	Mean
GDP/cap[a]	18,012	5,770	406	23,825
Growth[a]	0.031	0.011	406	0.020
Labor share[b]	0.61	0.50	352	0.54
Gini gross[c]	42.6	44.6	152	42.5
Gini net[c]	33.8	44.6	152	33.5

Note: The columns for 'Fell' cover the period until 2008, those for 'Now' cover the period 2008–14. Cell entries are means. *Sources*: (a) In PWT9.0 PPP dollars. (b) From PWT 9.0. (c) Gini coefficients of gross and net incomes, from SWIID (2014).

Moreover, there is nothing anti-democratic about people wanting to have a "strong" or "competent and effective" government – responses to survey questions that increased in frequency in recent years and which some commentators interpret as a symptom of declining support for democracy. Schumpeter (1942) certainly wanted governments to be able to govern and to govern competently, and I do not see why other democrats would not.

Yet we are nervous. We are nervous because we suspect that some of the conditions portrayed above are unprecedented, that extrapolations from history may be an unreliable guide to the current prospects. Are they unprecedented?

Table 8.1 compares the economic conditions of countries in which democracies fell or survived before 2008 with the post-2008 (and pre-2015) conditions of current democracies. Average incomes are now higher than even those of democracies that survived in the past. The average inequality of individual incomes mirrors that of surviving democracies. But labor share in manufacturing as well as growth of average incomes are lower.

These numbers, however, do not tell the full story. Consider first the stagnation of incomes of some percentage – between thirty and fifty – of people receiving the lowest incomes. Their incomes stagnated over almost forty years in the United States but only more recently in most European countries. In the United States the incomes of poorer people did not increase mainly because of increased inequality; in continental Europe the stagnation after 2008 was due princi- pally to slower growth. This stagnation is certainly unprece- dented during the period for which we have data on income distribution (1950 onwards), but perhaps even if we include the interwar period. The average rate of growth of the OECD- 2000 countries between 1978 and 2014 was 2.1 percent, while during the interwar period it was 2.3 percent. Yet inequality increased sharply during the recent period, while from the fragmentary information we have it seems that it declined quite significantly in the earlier period.[2] Hence, there are grounds to believe that lower incomes grew slower after 1978

---

[2] In the five countries for which we can calculate Gini coefficients of gross incomes during the interwar period, they decreased in France from forty- five in 1919 to forty in 1939, in Germany from thirty-eight in 1926 to thirty- five in 1932, in the Netherlands from forty-nine in 1919 to thirty-eight in 1939, in Sweden from forty-eight in 1919 to thirty-six in 1939, and in the United States from forty-four in 1919 to thirty-eight in 1939. These

than during the interwar period, which means that the current income stagnation of some bottom percentage of recipients is historically unprecedented, at least over the past one hundred years.

Particularly striking is the decline of unions, the opening gap between increases in productivity and of wage rates, which remain almost flat, and the decline of labor share in manufacturing. The power of unions to control the flow of labor to firms, conquered in several countries in the 1930s and institutionalized in the aftermath of World War II, has been eroding rapidly since the neo-liberal turn of the early 1980s, and weakening the political power of their electoral allies, the left-wing parties. This shift in the economic and political balance between capital and labor, coupled with a relaxation of control over capital flows and financial deregulation, resulted in the secular stagnation of incomes of lower-strata income recipients, punctuated by the crisis of 2008.

One should not be surprised, therefore, that beliefs in intergenerational equality are eroding. The 60 percent of respondents in the United States and 64 percent in Europe who believe that their children will be financially worse off than they are may be unduly pessimistic and still reacting to the shock of 2008, even though Chetty et al.'s (2016) evidence about the United States shows that these beliefs do not diverge far from reality. We do not have quantitative evidence about what previous generations believed, but there are good reasons to think that a belief in material progress has been deeply

calculations are based on transforming the Pareto coefficient o: provided by Atkinson, Piketty, and Saez (2011) into Gini coefficients.

ingrained in Western civilization since the industrial revolution. The average incomes among the OECD-2000 countries increased twenty-two-fold between 1820 and 2008. In spite of wars and economic crises, there was no thirty-year period in the past 200 years in which average incomes declined. So if people are now pessimistic about the future of their children, this may be a shift at a civilizational scale.

Whether the current polarization, accompanied by hostility with regard to people who hold different views, is new is impossible to judge. It is certainly new in the recent period but, as we have seen in the case studies of past crises, there have been periods in different countries, including the United States, when societies were deeply divided. All we know is that such intense divisions are long-lasting and difficult to overcome. They leave scars, which are often plastered by silence, as is the experience of the civil war in Spain or the divisions over Allende's period in Chile, and tend to resurge.

Finally, as confirmed in Table 8.2, perhaps the most dramatic recent change is the erosion of traditional party systems. The party systems that crystallized in Western Europe in the 1920s, with few exceptions, continued to constitute the main political alternatives until the end of the twentieth century. With the exception of the period immediately following World War II, voters had a choice between center-left and center-right. The parties representing these options, sometimes changing labels, splitting and merging, continued to be the two top vote-getters. New parties appeared from time to time but they were rarely successful and many were ephemeral. Of the two top vote-getters around 1924, 90 percent were still among the top two by the late 1990s,

Table 8.2 *Some political features of countries that were members of the OECD as of 2000, before and after 2008*

	1960–2007	1960–2007	2009–14	2009–14
	N	Mean	N	Mean
Turnout	1,065	78.8	138	72.1
Effparty in the electorate	1,065	4.05	137	4.68
Effparty in the legislature	1,065	3.48	137	3.86
Social democratic vote share	1,065	26.9	138	21.2
Union density	995	42.1	98	33.0

Note: Effparty is the effective number of parties.
Source: Armingeon et al. (2016).

but only about 75 percent are as of now. The number of "effective parties" was three in 1960 and it is almost four now. Moreover, this erosion has been accompanied by falling rates of electoral participation, with the share of radical Right parties increasing as turnout falls. It may be that this erosion is due to the loss of convocational power by the traditional parties or a shift of voters' preferences away from the center, as in the United States. Yet the decline of the traditional parties is not necessarily a reflection of an erosion of the political center. Rather, it may be a sign of their organizational weakness as well as a general disgust with professional politicians. All we can observe is that the traditional parties now come third, fourth, or even fifth in some countries, while in the United States a party that was once dominated by "Rockefeller Republicans" has been captured by the radical

Right. What is new is that both types of organizations that used to represent the working class – social democratic parties and trade unions – have lost this capacity. Both the social democratic vote shares and union density are distinctly lower in the most recent period. What has also changed, or at least is changing, is the social base of support for right-wing movements (Ignazi 1992, 2003, Arzheimer 2013). Traditionally such movements were supported by the petite bourgeoisie – self-employed, small shop-keepers, artisans, and farmers – while now they seek to combine this traditional base with appeals to the working class. As the social democratic parties became bourgeoisified, the right-wing parties became proletarianized.

The final but consequential difference between the past and the present, one that is encouraging, is that the military have pretty much disappeared from the political scene. The military played the decisive role in the collapse of nine out of fourteen democracies listed in Table 2.1. Indeed, had this text been written some forty years ago, the political stance of the military would have been its central preoccupation. Yet astonishingly it is no longer a political actor, even in Latin America, and it all but disappeared from the pages of political science as well.

Several caveats are in order to avoid unwarranted conclusions. Most importantly, the lessons from the past should not be treated as causal. Endogeneity is an obvious problem. As just one example: did democracies fall because the economies were stagnant or were the economies stagnant because democracies were about to fall? Second, the general patterns hide sharp differences among particular countries. Whatever global factors affect democracies, say worldwide economic depression, their effects work differently depending on the conditions specific to each country. Third, "difference" and "similarity" is a matter of degree and we do not know how much a particular difference matters. Finally, the list of conditions that we can observe is far from complete and it may well be that this list omits some that are crucial, alone or in combinations. Hence, as already stated, I am not trying to persuade the reader of anything but just provide food for thought. Drawing lessons from history is an art, not a science. What all of this adds up to – what the prospects are for democracy's survival under such conditions – one can only speculate about.

Part III

The Future?

Before we begin asking questions about possible futures, we
need to understand how democracy works when it works well
and how it collapses or deteriorates. Democracy functions well
when political institutions structure, absorb, and regulate
whatever conflicts may arise in society. Elections – the
mechanism by which a collectivity decides who should govern
it and how – are the central mechanism by which conflicts are
processed in democracies. Yet this mechanism functions well
only if the stakes are not very large, if losing an election is not
a disaster, and if the defeated political forces have a reasonable
chance to win in the future. When deeply ideological parties
come to office seeking to remove institutional obstacles in
order to solidify their political advantage and gain discretion
in making policies, democracy deteriorates, or "backslides."
This prospect is foreboding because the process need not entail
violations of constitutionality and, in turn, when backsliding
follows a constitutional path, when the government is careful
to preserve all appearances of legality, citizens have nothing
upon which to coordinate their resistance. Hence, it is reasonable to worry about whether it could happen in the United
States or in the mature democracies of Western Europe.

9

How Democracy Works

9.1 Conflicts and Institutions

The point of departure must be that at every moment in every society, some people – individuals, groups, or organizations – conflict over something. Often this something comprises various kinds of scarce goods, such as income, property, places at university, replacement organs, or access to public services. Many antagonisms, however, concern issues other than distribution. Some arise because some people have strong, often religiously motivated views about how others should act. Some are driven by a sheer desire for power, ambition, or vanity. Symbolic issues also evoke passions: in Weimar one government coalition broke over the issue of the colors of the German flag.

Not all antagonisms become political. Some of us are intensely divided by loyalty to different sport clubs, without such divisions becoming politicized. One woman may want to wear a burka on the beach and another nothing at all, but such discords may remain private. Even if some people have views about what others should or should not do, these are still private opinions. Antagonisms turn into political conflicts when they entail views about the policies governments should pursue and the laws they should adopt, most importantly about what governments should coerce all of us to do or not to do,[1] or when some groups attempt to impose their will over others by force, say in physically blocking access to abortion clinics or occupying someone else's property.

Conflicts may be easier or harder to resolve peacefully. They differ in several aspects:

1. How divided are people about what they want most to occur with regard to a particular issue? The answers to this question describe distributions of "ideal points": the policies or laws people see as best. One way to characterize such distributions is to ask whether there is some outcome that is preferred by more people than any other outcome and whether the proportion of people who like all other outcomes falls as the distance from the option preferred by most people increases. Distributions which satisfy both conditions are "unimodal." For example, the current distribution of attitudes toward abortion in the United States is unimodal, with more people opting for it being legal in most cases than in all cases, and more people opting for it being legal in most cases than illegal in most or all cases (Pew Research Center 2018). Yet it may well be that people's peak preferences concentrate around different outcomes. Some years ago in France, for example, a large segment of the population opposed same-sex marriage, fewer people wanted to allow it without the right to adopt, and another large segment supported it without

[1] Regulation of what women can or cannot wear on beaches has been in fact the subject of political conflicts in France. One long-standing conflict is whether people should be allowed to be nude on public beaches; the new one is whether they should be allowed to be clad from toe to head.

146

restrictions on adoption. This distribution was bimodal, as is the current United States distribution of postures on the general liberal–conservative dimension, shown in Figure 6.11. Interestingly, Medina (2015: figure 1) shows that voters' positions on the left–right dimension in twenty European countries tend to be trimodal (as Downs (1957) predicted), with a big mode at the center and smaller modes to the left and right of it.

2. How much do individuals care when outcomes deviate from their ideal preference? Clearly, people dislike more outcomes that are more distant from what they want most. But the intensity of their loss varies across issues as well as among individuals. Say that someone wants the top marginal tax rate to be 40 percent and the actual rate is 30 or 50 percent. This person views such tax rates as too low or too high, but this dissatisfaction is unlikely to be very intense. Yet for people who think that abortion should not be allowed under any circumstances, even legalizing the "morning-after" pill is anathema to them: their utility falls sharply when this is the law. Hence, even when the distribution of ideal points is unimodal, conflicts can be intense if people experience a sharp loss of utility when outcomes deviate even minimally from their peak preferences.

3. How closely related are positions on different issues? Are people who want abortion laws to be more restrictive the same as those who oppose immigration? Are people who oppose immigration the same as those who want more redistribution of income? If answers to these questions are positive, cleavages are superimposed; if they are

negative, cleavages are cross-cutting. For example, negative postures about immigration correlate with homopho-
bia and sexism across the OECD countries. Cleavages
tend to be superimposed when preferences are associated
with some other characteristics, say religion, income, or
education. According to the Pew survey cited above, for
example, only 25 percent of white Evangelicals agree to
abortion being legal under some circumstances, while
more than 50 percent of Catholics, about 70 percent of
traditional Protestants, and 75 percent of people unaffi-
liated with any religion do so. Because these groups differ
on other moral issues as well, cleavages are superimposed.
In turn, other cleavages may be cross-cutting: Lipset
(1960) has argued that the postures toward democracy
versus authoritarianism divide the working class, and we
have already examined the division between the SPD and
KPD in Weimar Germany.

It is reasonable to expect that conflicts are more
difficult to resolve peacefully when people's peak preferences
differ more, when the loss of utility associated with deviations
from these ideal preferences is more intense, and when cleavages are superimposed, clearly separating otherwise identifi-
able groups (Coser 1964). This is not to say that governments
are passive when confronting conflicts that are difficult to
manage. A natural strategy of governments is to try to persuade people that whatever divides them is less important
than what unites them. "Unity," as in "united we stand,"
"harmony," and "cooperation" are incessantly propagated
by appeals to nationalism, evocations of common roots even

in the face of divergent origins, celebrations of national holidays, anthems, and flags, expressions of pride in the national army or in the national performance in the Olympics – the list goes on. Even intensely divisive elections are always followed by a "unity" speech. To the best of my knowledge, Donald Trump was the first US president not to call for unity in his inaugural speech. Salvador Allende's declaration, "No soy Presidente de todos los Chilenos" (I am not the president of all the Chileans), was an enormous blunder.

It is hard to tell whether such exhortations have much effect, but the fact is that conflicts often persist in spite of them. Just for heuristic purposes, imagine that preferences can be placed on a single (utility) line, with a mass of people at points marked as A and B:

-- A ----- x ----- B --

Point x is a potential solution to the conflict. Say that point A represents the preference for a path to citizenship being open to all immigrants, illegal and legal; point B is the preference for deporting all illegal immigrants regardless of family considerations; and point x the preference for some intermediate solution, such as legalizing the status of parents whose children were born in the country. If A and B are sufficiently distant from each other on the utility scale, the conflict may have no solution. Say point x is unacceptable for people located at B and nothing farther from A than x is acceptable to people at A. Then the conflict has no solution acceptable to both groups. Think of the Chilean situation: not being able to nationalize some large firms in one stroke was unacceptable for the government coalition, only nationalizing firms one at a time was acceptable to the opposition. The Chilean conflict did not have a peaceful solution.

The same extends to more than one dimension. Remember that one large German party, the SPD, was socialist on the economic dimension and democratic on the political dimension, while another party, the DNVP, was capitalist and authoritarian. Because any majority coalition had to include both, the set of compromises that would be supported by a majority in the parliament was empty.

How, then, do we manage to process such conflicts in order and peace, without curtailing political freedom, relying on procedures and rules that indicate whose interests, values, or ambitions should prevail at a particular moment?

Political institutions orderly manage conflicts by (1) structuring conflicts, (2) absorbing conflicts, and (3) regulating them according to rules. An institutional order prevails if only those political forces that have institutionally constituted access to the representative system engage in political activities, and if these organizations have incentives to pursue their interests through the institutions and incentives to tolerate unfavorable outcomes. Specifically, conflicts are orderly if all political forces expect that they may achieve something, at the present or at least in some not too distant future, by processing their interests within this framework, while they see little to be gained by actions outside the institutional realm.

Note that thinking in strategic terms assumes that organizations can discipline the actions of their followers. As Maurice Thorez famously remarked in 1936, "One has to know how to end a strike." Organization, Pizzorno (1964) observed, is a capacity for strategy. Organizations can act strategically only if they can activate and deactivate their followers according to strategic considerations. When they do not have this capacity, political conflicts can assume the form of unorganized, "spontaneous" outbursts.

1. Political institutions structure conflicts. Institutions define the actions that particular actors can adopt, they provide incentives associated with each course of action, and constraints to the possible outcomes. As a result, they structure the actions which all actors would pursue given their interests or values and shape the collective outcomes, resulting in equilibria. Obviously, no one competes to conquer the office of the president in systems that have no such position: parliamentary monarchies. Only slightly less obvious is that the competition for the office of the president is more intense in systems where the president is the chief executive than in those in which he or she is only the ceremonial head of state. A more complicated example is the effect of electoral systems on electoral competition. With a single-district/single-member (SMD) system, and two parties, both parties have incentives to move toward the center of voters' preferences; with a high degree of proportionality, parties want to maximize their niche, which may lead some of them to maintain extreme postures. Such examples are endless.

Every political system molds the ways in which social forces organize as political actors, regulates the actions they can undertake, and constrains the policy outcomes that are subject to institutional competition. For example, rules according to which votes become transformed into legislative

151

seats – electoral systems – influence the number of parties that participate in electoral competition and the interests they represent: functional, regional, religious, ethnic, etc. Rules concerning unionization affect the number of trade union associations, their sectorial organization, and the extent of their centralization. Rules with regard to class actions determine whether only individuals or groups sharing the same grievance can address themselves to courts. Other rules define the actions that can be followed within the institutional framework. Most countries, for example, have laws regulating whether business lobbies and trade unions can financially support political parties. Most countries have laws defining which strikes are legal and which are not. Finally, constitutional courts or equivalent bodies can invalidate those outcomes that are inconsistent with some basic principles that stand above pluralistic competition, principles that are often but need not be enshrined in constitutions.

Political parties mold public opinion, compete in elections, and occupy executive and legislative offices. Parties became at one point the main form for organizing interests. They were a mechanism for articulating and aggregating interests, vertical organizations that integrated individuals into the representative institutions. For reasons that remain obscure, however, they transformed over time into organizations that function intermittently only at times of elections. They lost their socially integrative function: no one could say today with Michael Ostrogorskij (1981), "Do not convince them, take them in socially." Any kind of a daily, permanent connection is gone. And when parties do not have a day-to-day vertical connection with the people who end up supporting them at the time of elections, they cannot discipline their political actions.

Interest groups, whether lobbies of businesses, religious groups, or voluntary associations, seek to influence political parties as well as advance their interests by addressing themselves directly to the executive, including the lower echelons of the bureaucracy. One important difference in structuring conflicts lies in the area of regulation of functionally defined interests. Unions were banned in all European countries until the middle of the nineteenth century. Even when they were finally legalized, in all democracies the state tightly regulates the conditions under which they can be formed, whether one or multiple organizations can exist within a sector of industry or a particular workplace, whether collective agreements have the force of law, whether agreements concluded by unions apply to non-union members, etc. Note that, as shown in Figure 6.10, average union density declined sharply after about 1980, so that the power of union organizations over workers eroded similarly to that of political parties over their sympathizers. Lobbies of businesses are not equally tightly regulated, with only a few countries requiring that they register as such and make their activities transparent. Voluntary associations are regulated mainly through tax laws whenever they seek a not-for-profit status.

Civil law and its adjudication by courts individualize conflicts. Without recourse to courts many conflicts assume a form of spontaneous collective protests, as in China. But when individuals can direct their claims to courts, conflicts between them and the state become decentralized: in Argentina, for example, individuals sue the state in courts for not delivering services guaranteed in the constitution (Smulovitz 2003). Courts are a channel for processing conflicts without collective organization by the claimants.

In sum, states shape the organization of political forces that can appear on the terrain of political institutions. Other forms of political activity are either uneasily tolerated or actively repressed.

2. Institutions absorb political conflicts when those political forces which can potentially engage in other ways of promoting their interests or values have incentives to direct their actions within the institutional framework. What matters is not only whether they win or lose, but what can they win or lose: how much is at stake. A conflict over wages, for example, entails lower stakes than a strike over layoffs. The stakes in a conflict over dumping toxic waste into rivers may be low for industry, just involving somewhat lower or higher profits, and very high for those potentially exposed to the poison. The stakes in a decision to go to war may be enormous for everyone. Note that in many conflicts, the benefits of government decisions are concentrated, while the costs are diffuse: think of a tariff on toothpaste that significantly increases the profits of the producers and is almost imperceptible to the consumers. Conflicts that entail future political power entail high stakes because their outcomes are difficult to reverse. "Flexible labor market" policies, for example, may or may not reduce unemployment, but they undermine the organizational power of the unions and, thus, their chances to influence policies in the future.

Schematically, think about the fact that each organized political force expects to gain something by processing its interests within an institutional framework and has some idea about how reversible the outcome would be if it happens to lose, so that it has some notion of the expected value of participating in the institutional interplay of interests. The alternative that each political force faces is to use its resources outside the institutional framework, using violence or other inefficient forms of conflict processing (see below). This choice was starkly stated by John McGurk, chairman of the UK Labour Party in 1919: "We are either constitutionalists or we are not constitutionalists. If we are constitutionalists, if we believe in the efficacy of the political weapon (and we do, or why do we have a Labour Party?) then it is both unwise and undemocratic because we fail to get a majority at the polls to turn around and demand that we should substitute industrial action" (quoted in Miliband 1975: 69). His view, however, is not always shared: for example, the leader of a new left-wing political party in France, Jean-Luc Mélenchon, announced in the aftermath of his electoral defeat that he would lead his supporters to the streets. Moreover, one should not go too far in assuming that all such choices are dictated by strategic considerations. Each society has a fringe of fanatics, people who act without considering the consequences.

Both the resources that particular groups bring to the institutional interplay of interests and those they can mobilize for actions outside the institutional framework are group-specific. Multinational corporations have an effective lobbying power but no capacity to bring people to the streets. Unions may have less political influence but a damaging power to strike. The military are not supposed to have any institutional power but they are the ones who have arms. To be effective in absorbing conflicts, the power of particular actors within the institutional framework cannot diverge too much from their capacity to realize their objectives outside of it. Institutions function under the shadow of non-institutional power.

3. Institutions regulate conflicts if the losers accept outcomes determined by applying institutional rules. Political actors may use political institutions and still reject an unfavorable outcome. One may think, and some theorists do, that such situations are not possible. The argument is that if one group would adopt a strategy of "I will try within the institutions and if I fail I will go outside the institutions," then the group(s) with which it is in conflict would not direct their actions within the institutions, knowing that their institutional victory would be hollow. Hence, the argument goes, "if actors agree to some rules, they will obey them" or "if they do not intend to obey them, actors will not agree to the rules" (Buchanan and Tullock 1962, Calvert 1994). Yet we do witness situations in which a conflict should have been terminated according to some rules and still the losers do not accept the outcome, reverting to non-institutional actions. Collective agreements concluded by union organizations are sometimes rejected by rank-and-file workers, who engage in wildcat strikes. A legislature may pass a law that brings people to the streets in protest: educational reforms in France routinely mobilize massive opposition. Even election results are not always accepted by the losers: among democracies that fell,

this was the case in Honduras in 1932 and Costa Rica in 1958. The answer lies in uncertainty: outcomes of institutional interplay cannot be predicted exactly. Hence, a group may calculate *ex ante* that it would get something by directing its activities within the institutional framework, only to discover that it has lost, and that the resulting status quo is worse than what it can expect to get by going outside the institutional channels. In turn, the other group(s) may believe *ex ante* that a loss would be tolerable for their opponents, only to discover *ex post* that it is not.

One important aspect of institutions is whether they provide determinate rules according to which conflicts should be terminated. We have seen in the Chilean case, for example, that the legal framework contained two contradictory rules for treating the state monopoly of arms: on the one hand, the Congress passed the law giving jurisdiction over this monopoly to the military, empowering them to search for arms in government buildings; on the other hand, the law gave the president the authority not to allow the military to enter public buildings. Hence, the constitutional status of the search for arms became indeterminate, which undermined the posture of those generals who adhered to the principle of non-intervention as long as the president did not violate the constitution. Perhaps the most flagrant example of constitutional indeterminacy occurred in Ecuador in 1977, when three persons could claim with some justification that they were the president and the Supreme Court refused to arbitrate the conflict (Sanchez-Cuenca 2003: 78–9). Examples are many, but the general point is that sometimes constitutions and laws do not provide clear guidance for solving particular conflicts, and then the very distinction between institutional and non-institutional breaks down.

Given this characterization of conflicts and institutions, a question that naturally arises is whether all institutions can manage all conflicts in an orderly way. For example, some scholars think that a less proportional electoral system would have generated stable governments in Weimar Germany. Others, in turn, see the institutional culprit of Weimar in Article 48 of the constitution that allowed a president to appoint a government without the support of parliament and even in opposition to it (Bracher 1966: 119). Conversely, some scholars think that had Chile had a parliamentary instead of a presidential system, a center-right majority coalition would have been formed and democracy would have survived. One may also wonder what would have happened to democracy in France had the Fourth Republic continued rather than being replaced by a presidential system. Unfortunately, such claims must invoke counterfactuals, so they are inevitably speculative. We know enough about institutions to understand that, given the structure of political cleavages, some institutions could generate effective and stable governments while other institutions could not. Whether, however, a different institutional framework would have prevented the advent of Hitler to power or the fall of democracy in Chile is impossible to tell: too many contingencies are entailed.

The most important institution by which conflicts are processed in democracies are elections. Elections, however, are a peculiar way of processing conflicts, in that they occur on particular dates, are fixed independently of the current political situation in most countries, and are supposed to determine the relations of political power for some definite future. Political life, however, never stops. For one, the day an election is over, parties already begin to campaign for the next election. But politics between elections is not limited to electoral politics. The policies of governments elected by a majority may meet with opposition from groups that feel intensely about particular issues. Moreover, even if governments are elected by a majority, not all of the policies they propose need to enjoy majority support. Hence, we need to examine separately what happens in elections and what happens during the periods between elections.

9.2 Elections as a Method of Processing Conflicts

We select our governments through elections. Parties propose policies and present candidates, we vote, someone is declared to be winner according to pre-established rules, the winner moves into the government office, and the loser goes home. Glitches do sometimes occur, but mostly the process works smoothly. We are governed for a few years and then have a chance to decide whether to retain the incumbents or throw the rascals out. All of this is so routine that we take it for granted. What makes it possible?

Here is the puzzle stripped to its bare bones. Suppose that I want something that someone else wants as well; sometimes I want what is not mine. An application of some rule indicates that someone else should get it. Why would I obey this rule?

159

The very prospect that governments may change can result in a peaceful regulation of conflicts. To see this argument in its starkest form, imagine that governments are selected by a toss of a, not necessarily fair, coin: "heads" mean that the incumbents should remain in office, "tails" that they should leave. Thus, a reading of the toss designates "winners" and "losers." This designation is an instruction regarding what the winners and the losers should and should not do: the winners should move into a White, Blue, or Pink House or perhaps even a palace; while there they can take everything up to the constitutional constraint for themselves and their supporters; and they should toss the same coin again when their term is up. The losers should not move into the House and should accept not getting more than whatever they are given.

When the authorization to rule is determined by a lottery, citizens have no electoral sanction, prospective or retrospective, and incumbents have no electoral incentives to behave well while in office. Because electing governments through a lottery makes their chances of survival independent of their conduct, there are no reasons to expect that governments would act in a representative fashion because they want to earn re-election: any link between elections and representation is severed. Yet the very prospect that governments would alternate may induce the conflicting political forces to comply with the rules rather than engage in violence. Although the losers suffer temporarily by accepting the outcome of the current round, if they have a sufficient chance to win in future rounds they may prefer to comply with the verdict of the coin toss rather than revert to violence in the quest for power. Similarly, while the winners would prefer not to toss the coin again, they may be better off peacefully leaving office rather than provoking violent resistance to their usurpation of power. Examine the situation from the point of view of the losers in a particular election. They face the choice of either reverting to violence in order to grab power by force or accepting the cost of having lost and waiting to win the coin toss the next time around. What they will do depends on their chances of prevailing by force, on the cost of fighting, on the loss entailed by being governed against their will, and on their chances of winning the next time. This calculus may go either way, but they will wait so long as the policies imposed by the winners are not too extreme or so long as their chance to win at the next opportunity is sufficiently high. In turn, the winners know that to prevent the losers from rising in arms they have to moderate their policies or not abuse their incumbent advantage to deny the current losers the chance to win in the future. Regulating conflicts by a coin toss generates a situation in which peacefully waiting for one's chance may be best for each party given that the other party does the same. Bloodshed is avoided by the mere fact that the political forces expect to take turns.

Yet we do not use random devices; we vote. Voting is an imposition of a will over a will. When a decision is reached by voting, some people must submit to an opinion different from theirs or to a decision contrary to their interest. Voting generates winners and losers, and it authorizes the winners to impose their will, even if within constraints, on the losers. What difference does it make that we vote? One answer to this question is that the right to vote imposes an obligation to respect the results of voting. In this view, losers obey because they see it as their duty to obey outcomes resulting from a decision process in which they voluntarily participated. Outcomes of elections are "legitimate" in the sense that people are ready to accept the decisions of as-yet undetermined content so long as they can participate in the making of those decisions. I do not find this view persuasive, yet I think that voting does induce compliance, through a different mechanism. Voting constitutes "flexing muscles": a reading of chances in the eventual conflict. If all men are equally strong (or armed) then the distribution of votes is a proxy for the outcome of war. Clearly, once physical force diverges from sheer numbers, when the ability to wage war becomes professionalized and technical, voting no longer provides a reading of chances in a violent conflict. But voting does reveal information about passions, values, and interests. If elections are a peaceful substitute for rebellion, it is because they inform everyone who would mutiny and against what. They inform the losers – "Here is the distribution of force: if you disobey the instructions conveyed by the results of the election, I will be more likely to beat you than you will be able to beat me in a violent confrontation" – and the winners – "If you do not hold elections again or if you grab too much, I will be able to put up a forbidding resistance." Elections, even those in which incumbents enjoy an overwhelming advantage, provide some information about the chances of conflicting political forces in an eventual violent resistance. They reduce political violence by revealing the limits to rule.

In the end, elections induce peace because they enable intertemporal horizons. Even if one thinks that people care about outcomes rather than procedures, the prospect that parties sympathetic to their interests may gain the reins of government induces hope and generates patience. For many, the United States election of 2000 was a disaster, but we knew that there would be another one in 2004. When the 2004 election ended up even worse, we still hoped for 2008. And, as unbelievable as it still appears, the country that elected and re-elected Bush and Cheney, voted for Obama. Those who voted against Trump now hope he will be defeated in 2020. Elections are the siren of democracy. They incessantly rekindle our hopes. We are repeatedly eager to be lured by promises, to put our stakes on electoral bets. Hence, we obey and wait. The miracle of democracy is that conflicting political forces obey the results of voting. People who have guns obey those without them. Incumbents risk their control of governmental offices by holding elections. Losers wait for their chance to win office. Conflicts are regulated, processed according to rules, and thus limited. This is not consensus, yet not mayhem either. Just regulated conflict; conflict without killing. Ballots are "paper stones."

Yet this mechanism does not always work. Elections peacefully process conflicts if something is at stake in their outcomes, but not too much (Przeworski, Rivero, and Xi 2015). If nothing is at stake, if policies remain the same regardless of who wins, people observe that they voted in election after election, governments changed, and their lives remained the same. They may conclude that elections have no consequences and lose incentives to participate. The mirror danger occurs when too much is at stake, when having been on the losing side is highly costly to some groups and their prospects to be on the winning side in the future are dim, so that they see their losses as permanent or at least long-lasting. When incumbent governments make it next to impossible for the opposition to win elections, the opposition has no choice but to turn away from elections.

9.3 Government and Opposition Between Elections

An argument can be made that maintaining public order between competitive elections should not be problematic, precisely because the prospect of being able to win future elections is sufficient to induce the current losers to suffer in silence between elections. While O'Donnell (1994) diagnosed the reduction of politics to elections as a Latin American pathology, "delegative democracy," for James Madison this was how representative government should function: the people should elect governments but then have no role in governing. Lippman (1956) insisted that the duty of citizens, "is to fill the office and not to direct the office-holder." Schumpeter (1942) admonished voters that they "must understand that, once they elected an individual, political action is his business not theirs. This means that they must refrain from instructing him what he is to do."

As a description, this picture is obviously inaccurate (Manin 1997, 2017). Conflicts over policies are the bread and butter of everyday politics. Political activities are not limited to elections, nor even to efforts oriented toward influencing the outcomes of future elections. Moreover, while opposition to government policies can be limited to the institutional framework, under some conditions it spills outside of it.

The parliamentary opposition can stop or modify some actions of the government. If a policy proposed by the government is subject to legislative approval, the government may fail in parliament. Opposition parties may persuade government supporters to modify their views; they can exercise its institutional prerogatives to block some legislation (in Germany presidencies of parliamentary committees are distributed proportionately to party strength; in the United Kingdom the Committee of Public Accounts is by convention controlled by the opposition; in Argentina passing legislation requires a supermajoritarian quorum); they can threaten with obstructive tactics (a government proposal to privatize an electric utility company was met with thousands of amendments in France; filibustering in the United States Senate); they can threaten non-cooperation at the lower levels of governments they control. Note that if elections are expected to be competitive, the opposition faces a strategic choice of either accepting concessions from the government or going for broke with the hope of unseating the government in the next election. For example, in Brazil under the presidency of Fernando Henrique Cardoso, most parties were willing to support the government in exchange for pork barrel spending, but the Workers' Party (PT) invariably voted against the government and won the subsequent presidential election.

The opposition may also seek recourse to constitutional courts in order to restrict the actions of the government. Note that the logic of the role of elections in peacefully processing conflicts extends to the courts. Conflicting sides are willing to respect the verdicts of constitutional tribunals when they believe in their impartiality, specifically, that the tribunal considers each case on its merits. The losing side obeys the courts when it believes that in some future cases it may find itself to be the winner. When courts are blatantly partisan, this belief is eroded, and addressing conflicting issues to constitutional tribunals becomes futile.

Opposition, however, need not be limited to legislatures and courts. It can take place on the streets, in factories, or in offices. Street demonstrations are a standard repertoire of democratic opposition, as are strikes. As long as they are orderly and peaceful, they are just a routine tactic by which some groups signal their opposition to particular policies or their general dissatisfaction with the government. But demonstrations are not always peaceful: sometimes they are gratuitously repressed, sometimes they deteriorate into violence by marginal groups of demonstrators (they are called *casseurs*, "breakers" in France). The line between legal and illegal is thin. Hofstadter's (1969: 7) observation that "The normal view of governments about organized opposition is that it is intrinsically subversive and illegitimate" continues to be haunting. The idea that opposition to government policies does not need to signify treason or obstruction was first recognized in Great Britain in a parliamentary speech of 1828. But what kind of opposition is loyal and what kind subversive? Must opposition to government policies be channeled through the framework of representative institutions, or can people act in any way they please? Babasaheb Ambedkar, the father of the Indian constitution, thought that while civil disobedience was appropriate under colonial rule, it is "nothing but the Grammar of Anarchy" under democracy. In the words of David Cameron, the former British prime minister, demonstrations by students against raising tuition fees "were a part of democracy but violence and law-breaking was not" (BBC News). Actions such as blocking roads and bridges, occupying buildings, lock-outs, civil disobedience, rioting, and in the extreme terrorism, are intended to undermine the government by undermining public order. Moreover, violence is not always directed against governments. We have seen that in many instances private groups, sometimes organized as paramilitary organizations but sometimes just forming spontaneously, engage in violence against each other: this was the case in Weimar Germany and Chile, as well as in the United States during the 1960s.

Demonstrations that end in violence, violent labor conflicts, blockages of roads and bridges, occupations of buildings, lock-outs, civil disobedience, street fights, riots, and terrorism are what I mean by conflicts spilling outside the institutional boundaries. They constitute breakdowns of public order. They are costly to the perpetrators, to the government, and often to third parties. They may occur as a result of strategic decisions of some groups but they may also erupt spontaneously.

Consider a situation in which a government has the monopoly of legislative initiative and is assured of the support of a majority in the legislature. All bills are initiated by the executive and all the bills become laws. Moreover, the government acts with full legality or the courts are partisan, so any recourse to the judicial system would be futile. Examine this situation from the point of view of a social group opposed to a particular policy. This group has no chance of influencing government policy within the institutional system: the government wants to adopt the policy, the legislature is just a rubber stamp and offers no recourse. The most this group can expect of the system of representative institutions is that if the policy turns out to be sufficiently unpopular, the government would lose the next election and the policy would be reversed. But suppose that in addition, the government has a good chance of being re-elected. Then this group has nothing to gain by acting within the institutional framework. Under such conditions it may be sufficiently desperate to try stopping the policy by acting outside the institutional channels.

Saiegh generated interesting information relating the rate at which bills proposed by the executive are approved as laws by legislatures ("Box score" in Figure 9.1) and the incidence of riots. Governments do not always get what they want in the legislatures: according to Saiegh (2009), democratic legislatures approved only 76 percent of bills proposed by the executive during the 783 country years for which these data are available. In turn, under democracy (Saiegh's regime classification is based on Alvarez et al. 1996), riots are more frequent when the executive is either not at all effective or when the legislature is just a rubber stamp.

I interpret these patterns as saying that institutions are successful in regulating conflicts when the government is sufficiently able to govern but the opposition has an important voice in policy making. Politics spills out of institutional bounds either when governments are too weak to be able to pass legislation or so strong that they do not need to

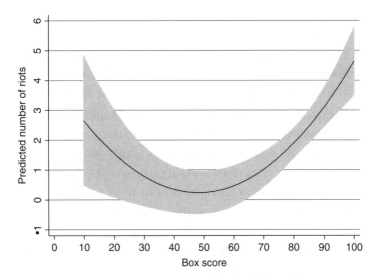

Figure 9.1. Proportion of bills passed and riots
Source: Saiegh (2009)

accommodate legislative opposition. As several French politicians commented in the aftermath of President Macron's
massive legislative victory, "if the debate does not take place in
the parliament, it will occur on the streets."

Breakdowns of public order tend to spiral.
Historical experience suggests that when conflicts spill
onto the streets, public support for authoritarian measures
designed to maintain public order tends to increase, even
when protests are targeted precisely against the authoritarian tendencies of governments. People do expect governments to maintain order; indeed, no society can tolerate
permanent disorder. Protracted public transportation
strikes or strikes causing shortages, road blockages, or

other actions that paralyze everyday life provoke a backlash even among the people who are sympathetic to the cause of strikers. Repeated street fights induce the atmosphere of disorder and insecurity. Hence, governments are always tempted to portray actions against them as illegal. Particularly dangerous are "situations in which the authorities, the police, and the judiciary, even if disapproving of violent political acts, dealt leniently with them because they felt sympathetic to the motives of those engaging in them or hostile to their victims" (Linz 1978: 57). In turn, in such political climates the repressive forces, whether ordinary or riot police, feel authorized to use violence even in the face of peaceful protests: think of the "police riot" during the 1968 Chicago Democratic Party convention. When these forces are not well trained and disciplined, tragic accidents are almost inevitable: think of the massacre of students at Kent State University on May 4, 1970. And when peaceful actions are brutally repressed, some people conclude that they are being pushed out of the institutional framework and revert to terrorism, as in the United States, Germany, and Italy in the 1960s–1970s.

I do not claim that these are regular patterns: we know little that is systematic about dynamics of disorder and repression. The only conclusion one can draw from these examples is that breakdown of public order is something which all governments must fear. Faced with demonstrations that turn violent, road blockages, protracted transportation strikes, or fights between private groups, governments have only two choices: either to persevere with their policies while reverting to repression or to abandon their policies in order to placate the opposition. Neither alternative is attractive. The spirals of unrest and repression undermine public order, while repeated concessions render governments unable to implement any stable policies.

9.4 How Democracies Fail

Democracy works well when representative institutions structure conflicts, absorb them, and regulate them according to rules. Elections fail as a mechanism for processing conflicts either when their outcomes have no consequences for people's lives or when incumbents abuse their advantage to the point of making them non-competitive. Once elected, governments must be able to govern, but they cannot ignore the views of intense minorities. When conflicts are intense and a society is highly polarized, finding policies acceptable to all major political forces is difficult and may be impossible. Miscalculations, whether by governments or different groups opposing them, lead to institutional breakdowns. When governments ignore all opposition to their policies, when they interpret all opposition as subversive, when they engage in gratuitous repression, they push the opposing groups out of the institutional framework: opposition turns into resistance. When some groups of the opposition refuse to accept policies resulting from applying the institutional rules, governments may have no choice but to engage in repression to maintain public order. Finding the right balance between concession and repression is a subtle choice. Failures are inevitable.

10

Subversion by Stealth

10.1 Democratic Backsliding

The dream of all politicians is to remain forever in office and to use their tenure to do whatever they want. Most democratic governments attempt to advance these goals by building popular support within the established institutional framework. Some, however, seek to protect their tenure in office and to remove obstacles to their discretion in choosing policies by undermining institutions and disabling all opposition. Prominent recent examples are Turkey under the government of the Justice and Development Party (AKP), Venezuela under Chavez and Maduro, Hungary under the second government of Fidesz, and Poland under the second government of PiS.

Democratic "deconsolidation" or "backsliding" is a process of gradual erosion of democratic institutions and norms. Ginsburg and Huq (2018a: 17) use the term "authoritarian retrogression," distinguished from outright "reversion," and define it as "a process of incremental (but ultimately still substantial) decay in the three basic predicates of democracy – competitive elections, liberal rights to speech and association, and the rule of law." As "backsliding" or "deconsolidation" or "retrogression," whatever one wants to call it, advances, the opposition becomes unable to win elections or assume office if it wins, established institutions lose the capacity to control the executive, and manifestations of popular protest are repressed by force. This process is propelled by the desire of a government to monopolize power and to remove obstacles to realizing its ideal policies. Yet it is a process of interaction between the government and various actors that seek to block it. Hence, the strategy of the governments that go down this path concentrates on disabling potential blockers, who differ from case to case but typically include the opposition parties, the judicial system, and the media, as well as the streets.

Think about it as follows. A government deeply committed to a particular ideological goal – such as Islamization in Turkey, "Bolivarianism" in Venezuela, "preserving the purity of the nation" in Hungary, or "defending Christianity" in Poland – wins an election.[1] This government decides whether to take steps to increase its ability to remain in office or steps that would increase its discretion in policy making. As Lust and Waldner (2015: 7) put it, "Backsliding occurs through a series of discrete changes in the rules and informal procedures that shape elections, rights and

[1] The definition of "victory" is not as simple as it may appear. Electoral laws play an important role: in Turkey, the AKP won 34.3 percent of votes to obtain 66 percent of seats when it first assumed power in 2002, in Hungary Fidesz won 53 percent of votes and 68 percent of seats in 2010, in Poland PiS got 37.5 percent of votes and 51 percent of seats. The ascension of Chavez to office in Venezuela was convoluted: the traditional parties actually won the legislative election of 1998, Chavez won the presidential election with 56.4 percent, the referendum for a new constitution was passed by 71.8 percent, then Chavez won a new election with 59.8 percent while his party obtained 44.4 percent of the votes and 55.7 of the seats in the legislative election of 2000.

accountability. These take place over time, separated by months or even years." Examples of the first kind of steps include changing electoral formulae, redistricting, changing voting qualifications (age, eligibility of citizens residing abroad), harassing the partisan opposition, or imposing restrictions on non-governmental organizations. Examples of the second kind of steps include shifting power from the legislature to the executive, reducing the independence of the judicial system, or using referendums to overcome constitutional barriers. Some measures, such as instituting constitutional reforms, imposing partisan control over state apparatuses, or controlling the media, have both effects. Having observed such steps, citizens who value democracy may turn against the government even if they support its policies or enjoy outcomes which they attribute to its policies. If the opposition rises, the government may be removed from office or it may decide to stop taking further steps, anticipating its rise.

In principle, the opposition could prevent governments from taking the next step either by stopping it by legal measures, such as defeating a bill in parliament, or obtaining a presidential veto or favorable court ruling. The history of the four cases we referred to above shows, however, that governments regularly overcome legal obstacles. In Turkey, when in 2007 the president vetoed a constitutional amendment passed by the parliament for direct election of the president, the government organized a referendum and won. In Venezuela, when the opposition won a legislative election in December 2015, Maduro replaced the Congress with a newly elected Constitutional

Assembly. In Hungary, when the Constitutional Tribunal invalidated an electoral reform in 2013, the government passed a constitutional amendment curbing the power of the tribunal. In Poland, when the president vetoed two laws concerning the courts, he was quickly persuaded to change his mind. This is not to say that governments always prevail: in Poland, for example, the government withdrew from fining an opposition TV station that is owned by US interests. Nevertheless, it seems that legal counter-moves by the opposition at most slow down the process but are ineffective in stopping it. This is why we think of the opposition in terms of an effective threat to removing the government and reversing the process of democratic deterioration.

The obvious question is why some governments decide to go down this path while most refrain from it. The second is whether, once a government takes such steps, it can ever be stopped short of the realization of complete domination while still remaining in office. The third is whether the potential opposition would be able to remove the government and reverse this process.

It bears emphasis that we try to understand the "how" rather than the "when": how does deconsolidation evolve when it does, rather than under what conditions it is likely to occur. We learn from the experiences of the four countries mentioned above – we sample on the dependent variable – because we want to understand how democracies can be destroyed by small steps, not why backsliding occurs in some countries and not in others, for which see Maeda (2010), Svolik (2015), and Graham, Miller, and Strøm (2017).

Our question is not "Will it happen here?" but "Can it happen anywhere?"

10.2 Stealth

The puzzle entailed in the destruction of democracy by "backsliding" is how a catastrophic state of the world can be gradually brought about by small steps, against which people who would be adversely affected do not react in time. As Ginsburg and Huq (2018b: 91) pose it, "The key to understanding democratic erosion is to see how discrete measures, which either in isolation or in the abstract might be justified as consistent with democratic norms, can nevertheless be deployed as mechanisms to unravel liberal constitutional democracy." In the parable of "the frog in the pot," if a frog is put suddenly into hot water, it will jump out, but if it is put in cold water which is then heated slowly, it will not perceive the danger and will be cooked to death. Yet the parable is not true: recent experiments show that the frog will get uncomfortable when the water is heated and will try to jump out (see "Boiling Frog" on Wikipedia). How, then, can gradual backsliding succeed in destroying democracy?

The first lesson we are learning from recent experiences is that democracies do not contain institutional mechanisms that safeguard them from being subverted by duly elected governments observing constitutional norms. When Hitler came to power, through an "authoritarian gap in the Weimar Constitution" (Article 48, which allowed the president to empower the government to rule by decree; Bracher 1966: 119), the possibility of a legal path to dictatorship was seen as a flaw of this particular constitution. Yet such gaps may be generic. The father of constitutionalism, Montesquieu (1995: 326), insisted that "For the abuse of power to be impossible, it is necessary that by the disposition of things, the power stop the power." But, *pace* Madison (Federalist #51), checks and balances do not operate effectively when different powers of the government are controlled by the same party: as Madison himself was almost immediately to discover (Dunn 2004: 47–61), the constitutional separation of powers is vulnerable to partisan interests. Courts, constitutional as well as ordinary, can be packed, intimidated, or circumvented. Wholesale changes of constitutions, amendments, or referendums can constitutionally overcome extant constitutional obstacles. Public bureaucracies, including security agencies, can be instrumentalized for partisan purposes. Public media can be controlled by partisan regulatory bodies, while private media can be legally intimidated or destroyed financially. All such measures can be taken legally. As Landau (2013: 192–3) observes, "The set of formal rules found in constitutions is proving to be a mere parchment barrier against authoritarian and quasi-authoritarian regimes. There is even worse news: existing democracy-protecting mechanisms in international and comparative constitutional law have proven ineffective against this new threat."

Democratic deconsolidation need not entail violations of constitutionality. Thinking about the United States, a constitutional lawyer writes,

> If it happens here, it won't happen all at once ... Each step might be objectionable but not, by itself, alarming ... there

> will have been no single, cataclysmic point at which
> democratic institutions were demolished ... the steps
> toward authoritarianism will not always, or even usually,
> be obviously illegal ... In fact, each step might conform to
> the letter of the law. But each step, legal in itself, might
> undermine liberal democracy a little bit more. (Strauss
> 2018: 365–6)

In a broader context, another constitutional lawyer concludes that "it is difficult to identify a tipping point during the events: no single new law, decision or transformation seems sufficient to cry wolf; only ex-post do we realize that the line dividing liberal democracy from a fake one has been crossed: threshold moments are not seen as such when we live in them" (Sadurski 2018: 5). This is what we mean by "stealth": "the use of legal mechanisms that exist in regimes with favorable democratic credentials for anti-democratic ends" (Varol 2015).

In turn, when the government takes steps that are not flagrantly unconstitutional or undemocratic, citizens who benefit from its policies but still value democracy are not certain how to react. Some measures that backsliding governments adopt do not even require legal acts, just a change of practices. For example, the Polish ruling party, PiS, gradually altered the parliamentary procedure concerning the introduction of new bills: the parliamentary rules say that bills proposed by the government must be subject to public hearings, while private member bills are not, and the government shifted to offering its proposal as private bills of its deputies (Sadurski 2018: 6). Moreover, nothing is constitutionally wrong with legal measures such as a parliamentary act easing restrictions on the teaching of the Koran (June 2005 in Turkey), anti-terror laws (June 2006 in Turkey, May 2016 in Poland), or a statute that requires non-governmental organizations to register as foreign organizations if they receive funding from abroad (June 2017 in Hungary). These are ordinary laws, passed according to constitutional provisions by the legally competent bodies, a prerogative of any democratic government. Even changes of constitutions are valid so long as they observe constitutional provisions, as they did in Hungary in April 2011, and in Turkey after the referendums of October 2007 (direct election of the president, after the incumbent president vetoed a parliamentary act), September 2010 (increased civilian control over the military and the courts), and April 2011 (introducing a presidential system). As a result, several observers agree, "there is usually no single event or governmental conduct which may mobilize the resistance by sending a clear signal that democratic norms are imperilled" (Ginsburg and Huq, 2018a), "slow slides towards authoritarianism often lack both the bright spark that ignites an effective call to action and the opposition and movement leaders who can voice that clarion call" (Bermeo 2016: 14).

Protests against legal measures taken by a government that just won an election only show that the opposition is a sore loser, that it does not respect democratic norms. Even more perverse are the situations in which governments succeed in packing or controlling the constitutional tribunals and then use judicial review to legitimize their actions, as they did in Venezuela, Turkey, and Hungary. They are perverse because they allow governments to portray actions of the opposition as anti-constitutional: in President Trump's tweet the appointment of Special Counsel Robert Mueller was "totally UNCONSTITUTIONAL" (@realDonaldTrump June 4, 2018 at 4.01 p.m.). Part of the rhetorical games entailed in backsliding is to compete for the mantle of "democracy" and "constitutionalism," in which the opposition does not always prevail. Thus a pro-Putin Russian journalist, Mikhail Leontiev, disingenuously observes: "I do not understand what is undemocratic in that some force enjoying overwhelming social support wins elections" (an interview with a Polish newspaper, *Dziennik*, January 19, 2008).

Note that claims of "unconstitutional" in principle require a more rigorous test than claims of "undemocratic." Declarations that a particular statute or an action of the government violates the constitution are issued by specialized bodies designated by a constitution and are couched as interpretations of its text. But courts are populated bodies (Ferejohn and Pasquino 2003): their decisions are made by particular people, appointed by politicians. Hence, if a government succeeds in stuffing these bodies with its partisan supporters, they issue decisions favorable to the government. Venezuela is a flagrant example. Moreover, constitutions can be amended or completely replaced, still by constitutional provisions. Even when the extant constitution is entrenched, the entrenchment clauses can be modified to enable constitutional change.

True, constitutionality can be questioned even when a court is constitutionally formed and when it rules that actions of the government are constitutional. One issue is whether an act adopted following constitutional provisions that abrogates constitutionality altogether can ever be considered as constitutional. The prominent example is the

German Enabling Act (*Gesetz zur Behebung der Not von Volk und Reich*) of March 24, 1933 that gave the government the power to act in an extra-constitutional way: "In addition to the procedure prescribed by the constitution, laws of the Reich may also be enacted by the government of the Reich" (Article 1). A literal interpretation of "constitutionality" does not provide a decisive criterion. Some broader conception must be invoked to deem actions of a government as violating constitutionality when the pertinent bodies declare them to be constitutional. Thus Landau (2013: 195) considers "the use of mechanisms of constitutional change in order to make a state significantly less democratic than it was before" as "abusive constitutionalism," while the Colombian Constitutional Court ruled that even duly adopted constitutional amendments can be unconstitutional (Ginsburg and Huq 2018b: 188). Given that such conceptions are inescapably vague, partisan-based disagreements are inevitable.

The notion of "undemocratic" is even more permissive. There is nothing "undemocratic" about the election of Donald Trump: in the words of his advertisement, "Our movement is about replacing a failed and corrupt political establishment with a new government controlled by you, the American people."[2] It is even more paradoxical to claim the same about referendums, in which Marine Le Pen, advocating a vote on "Frexit," promised "You, the people, will decide." Not holding scheduled elections or committing blatant fraud are almost universally seen as violations of democratic norms, but short of this

---

[2] See www.youtube.com/watch?v=vST61W4bGm8.

instinctive marker the norms of what constitute undemocratic practices are less crystallized and diverge even more across partisan lines. For example, in the United States almost everyone believes that fraud-free elections with equal voting rights are important for democracy, but fewer people think that it is important that districts not be biased or that the government not interfere with the press, with divergence between supporters and opponents of President Trump (Bright Line Watch 2018).

Moreover, it is often controversial whether some steps taken by governments are anti-democratic. Imagine that a government extends voting rights to citizens residing abroad (Erdoğan did it, but also Berlusconi), or it adopts legislation to require additional documentation at the polling place, or it remaps electoral districts. Are these steps antidemocratic? The government says "We want to extend rights to all citizens," "We want to prevent fraud," "We want every vote to have equal weight." The opposition says "The government does not care about rights and is extending the vote to Turks in Berlin only because they will vote for it," "The government does not care about fraud, it only wants to prevent poor people, who do not have the documents, from voting," "The government is redistricting in its favor." All these steps are adopted following constitutional provisions, so they are not "undemocratic" in the sense of violating procedural norms. The disagreements are not about facts but about intentions and intentions are not directly observable.

Now, governments may take actions that are flagrantly unconstitutional or undemocratic. Refusing to comply with court rulings is clearly unconstitutional and in the United States makes the perpetrator subject to contempt-of-court charges. Banning an opposition newspaper flagrantly violates democratic norms. Moreover, some are offensive whether or not they are either: shooting peaceful demonstrators, as at Kent State University on May 4, 1970, may provoke widespread outrage whatever the legal or normative niceties. Stealth is a process by which the government takes certain steps, none of which is flagrantly unconstitutional or undemocratic, and which cumulate in undermining the capacity of the opposition to remove it or enlarge its discretion in making policies.

10.3 Dynamics of Subversion from Above

"Parchment barriers" are not sufficient to prevent the erosion of democracy by governments that proceed by stealth. The question, then, is whether a government intent on backsliding can be dissuaded from pursuing it or be removed because of the rise of popular opposition.

Suppose that at each moment the government decides whether to take a step that increases its incumbent advantage or brings the policy closer to its ideals or both, anticipating the size of the opposition to such steps. In turn, individual citizens decide whether to turn against the government or to support it, perhaps waiting to see if the government would continue taking additional steps. The probability that the government remains in office depends on the number of steps it takes to protect its tenure from the potential opposition and on the size of the opposition. The more such steps the government successfully takes, the larger the opposition required to generate the same chance of removing it. The government enters the backsliding path if taking some steps will make it better off in terms of staying in office and implementing its preferred policies than the institutional status quo. It stops if the gain from taking further steps is outweighed by the danger of increased opposition. At each step it may be removed from office according to the probabilities described above.

Individuals attach different weights to the extent to which they care about democracy and about some policies, such as anti-immigration measures, or outcomes, such as income growth (Svolik 2017, Graham and Svolik 2018). People who do not like the outcomes the government generates, say environmentalists under the Trump government, oppose it regardless of the value they place on democracy. In turn, people who support government policies trade off their benefits from policies against the damage to democracy at different rates, where "democracy" means that the government can be removed by elections (or some constitutional provisions, such as impeachment or a vote of non-confidence), when a sufficient majority opposes it. Obviously, there may be people who do not care about democracy at all.

While this much is general, there are many possibilities. The opposition may not rise at all; it may remain dormant at first and only then suddenly increase; it may remain at some constant level or just rise sporadically in reaction to particular measures of the government. Given that by making appropriate assumptions one can obtain any result one wants, to generate conclusions by assuming them, we keep these possibilities as open as possible by exploring the generic conditions under which a government enters on the path of deconsolidation, as well as the conditions, if any, under which it ever stops under the threat of opposition, or is removed from office while deconsolidating.

The central conclusion[3] is that everything depends on whether people who are at all concerned about democracy anticipate the effects of particular steps on the long-term future. If individuals anticipate the cumulative effect of backsliding, those who value democracy would turn rapidly against the backsliding government and, expecting this reaction, a government intent on backsliding would desist from taking or continuing far on this path. This would be true even if people were uncertain to begin with whether the government intends to backslide and would update their beliefs about the type of government they face only when the government takes some steps. In turn, if individuals react only to their current situation, the opposition rises too slowly to prevent a government intent on backsliding from taking a sufficient number of steps to secure its incumbent advantage and to remove institutional obstacles to its discretion in making policy. The opposition rises somewhat faster if some policy measures of a backsliding government would be also taken by a democratic one, and it rises somewhat slower if individuals are uncertain whether the particular steps are intended to increase incumbent advantage, but neither possibility prevents the government from backsliding. Hence,

---

[3] The conclusions are based on a series of mathematical models developed jointly with Zhaotian Luo. See Luo and Przeworski (2018).

unless people react at the onset against actions by the government that would have a cumulative effect of eroding democracy, democracy erodes.

Defending democracy imposes a difficult, perhaps impossible, challenge for individual citizens. To act now against the government that may in some future destroy democracy, individuals who currently enjoy its policies or some outcomes which they attribute to policies[4] must see the long-term effect of current policies. Even if individuals have consistent time preferences (Akerlof 1991), and even if they are concerned about the future, they must be able to calculate the cumulative effect of particular, seemingly democratic steps — they must be able to see through the stealth. This is a formidable task and, even if the incapacity to anticipate the future violates the assumption of full rationality, it should not be surprising if people cannot perform it. Consider a sequence of events in which the government first adopts legislation to require additional documentation at the polling place, then has its cronies buy an opposition newspaper, then remaps electoral districts, and then controls the bodies that administer and supervise elections. What people need to see is that, while each of these measures may have little effect, their cumulative effect is to protect the incumbent from being defeated even by a largely majoritarian opposition. Moreover, policies have

---

[4] Note that in Turkey per capita incomes grew at the annual rate of 4.4% under the AKP government, Venezuela enjoyed spectacular growth between 2004 and 2011 (except for 2009) due to oil prices, Hungary grew at the rate of 3.5% under Fidesz, and Polish incomes continued to grow under PiS. (Data from PWT 9.0, ending in 2014.)

interactive effects that are even more difficult to calculate: Sheppele's (2013) example is the interaction of Article 48 of the Weimar Constitution, that permitted the president to declare a state of emergency, subject to the check that parliament could reject such a declaration, and Article 25 that permitted the president to dissolve the parliament once for any reason, the effect of which was that once parliament was dissolved, the president could declare an emergency at will. Even the most competent constitutionalists, who authored this constitution, did not see the potential effects of this combination, and it proved fatal.

One might think that people would be educated to look toward the long-term future by leaders of the opposition. But their potential role is limited. Exhortations by partisan opposition are not likely to be effective in influencing beliefs. People know that the goal of the leaders of the opposition is to replace the incumbents, whether they act for good or bad reasons. If opposition leaders criticize every action of the government, people tend to dismiss their messages: as Austen-Smith (1992) put it, speech that is predictable according to interests is not credible. And if only the extreme opponents of the government turn out on the streets, the government can claim that the opposition is undemocratic, and others are less likely to join (Shadmehr and Berhardt 2011).

The fact is that backsliding governments have enjoyed continued popular support. To the best of my knowledge, the only case in which a backsliding government lost an election and left office is in Sri Lanka in 2015, and this outcome resulted from massive defections from the ruling coalition, with the winner previously being a minister in the outgoing government. Other backsliding governments have suffered temporary reversals but were able to recover and continue: with 40.9 percent of votes, the AKP failed to win a majority of seats in the election of June 7, 2015, but it called for a new election and won 49.5 percent of the vote five months later. Three years later, in June 2018, Erdoğan won the presidential election with 52.6 percent. In Poland, a majority of survey respondents thought that the government was "performing badly" when it began to tinker with the Constitutional Court in 2015, but the government was positively evaluated by a majority two years later, by October 2017 (Kantar Public 2018). In Hungary, Fidesz and its allies won re-election in April 2018 with 44.9 percent of the vote. In Venezuela, Chavez won re-election in 2006 with 62.8 percent of the vote and again in 2,102 with 55.1 percent. He enjoyed majority support in the polls and the opposition became majoritarian only after his death (Venezuelabarometro). And in the United States, the popularity of President Trump hovers narrowly around 40 percent regardless of anything. The implication must be that either many people do not care at all about democracy or that they do not see the long-term consequences for democracy when they vote or answer survey questions.

10.4 Could It Happen Here?

All conclusions must be speculative. Intentions matter, determination to pursue them matters, resistance is effective only when it is optimally timed and sustained, and the conditions under which the opposition rises are difficult to satisfy. But the optimism that citizens would effectively threaten governments that commit transgressions against democracy and thus prevent them from taking this path (Montesquieu 1995: book 19, chapter 19, Weingast 1997, 2015, Fearon 2011) is sadly unfounded. Montesquieu had hoped that if power were to be abused, "everything would [be] united against it," there would be a revolution, "which would not change the form of government or its constitution: for revolutions shaped by liberty are but a confirmation of liberty." Yet these views are based on the assumption that the government commits some acts that flagrantly threaten liberty, violate constitutional norms, or undermine democracy. But when a government proceeds by stealth, citizens turn against it only if they see what its actions are leading to in the long run. Hence, resistance against a backsliding government imposes a difficult challenge on individual citizens. The effect of stealth is to obscure the long-term danger. And if the opposition does not stop the government from taking some series of legal steps, it will be too late to prevent it from taking illegal ones.

Can it happen anywhere? Could it happen in the United States? Here is a nightmare scenario.

First: Congress passes a law prohibiting the publication of "false, scandalous, and malicious writings against the government of the United States, the Congress, or the President, with intent to bring them into contempt or disrepute" (Sedition Act of 1798; in Stone: 2018: 491) or those using "disloyal, profane, scurrilous, or abusive language" about the United States government, its flag, or its armed forces or that caused others to view the American government or its institutions with contempt. Those convicted under the act will receive sentences of imprisonment for five to twenty years (Sedition Act of 1918).

Next: the Supreme Court grants large discretion to state legislatures in designing districting plans.

Next: Congress passes a law, according to which making public official documents without the authorization of the government agency is subject to fines or imprisonment. "[T]he Constitution imposes little constraint on the selective disclosure (or nondisclosure) of information by the state in ways that can shunt public debate away from questions that would embarrass or undermine political leaders" (Ginsburg and Huq 2018b: 67).

Next: Congress passes a law against electoral fraud, mandating states to adopt rules concerning documents required to register to vote.

Next: the number of federal judges nominated by the administration reaches 112 (the total number of vacancies to be filled before 2020).

Next: the president issues an executive order decreeing that "all persons privileged to be employed in the departments and agencies of the Government, shall be reliable, trustworthy, of good conduct and character," and should demonstrate "unswerving loyalty to the United States" (Executive Order 10450 of President Eisenhower in 1953, quoted in Goldsmith 2018: 106). Hundreds of civil servants appointed before 2016 are purged.

Next: Congress passes a law withdrawing tax-exempt status from non-governmental organizations which "obstruct the implementation of duly adopted laws and regulations."

Next: two Supreme Court justices are replaced by administration nominees.

Next: Congress passes a new anti-terrorism law according to which anyone who "threatens national security" is subject to preventive detention. "[Y]ou are kidding yourself if you think the same thing will not happen again. Because Inter arma enim silent leges . . . in times of war, the laws fall silent" (Justice Scalia, referring to Korematsu vs United States, quoted in Minow 2018: 321).

Next: the president is re-elected.

Next: the president issues a series of executive orders on issues previously subject to legislation. Congress remains mute. The Supreme Court remains mute.

The fat lady sings.

11

What Can and Cannot Happen?

> I will disclose to you what raised me to my position. Our
> problems seemed complicated. The people did not know
> what to do about them. In these circumstances people
> preferred to leave them to the professional politicians. I, on
> the other hand, have simplified the problem and reduced
> them to the simplest formula. The masses recognized this
> and followed me. (Adolf Hitler, quoted in Linz 1978: 53–4)

As J.K. Galbraith once remarked, "The only function of economic forecasting is to make astrology look respectable."
Making political predictions is even more hazardous.
Uncertainty is inherent under any circumstances and it is
exceptionally high when big issues are at stake and conflicts
are intense. Hence, the best we can perhaps achieve is to
identify the range of possibilities contained in the current crisis.

The most optimistic scenario in the economic realm is
that the crisis – the stagnation of lower incomes, job insecurity,
and the erosion of beliefs in intergenerational mobility – will just
blow over and, to the extent that the political discontent is driven
by the economy, so will the political impasse. Growth is accel-
erating in developed countries, with average incomes finally
surpassing the pre-2008 levels. Unemployment has declined
from post-2008 levels. Globalization, specifically the outflow of
jobs to low-wage countries, is slowing down. Wages in China
have increased 64 percent in five years, even if they remain low in
other countries. The rates of return to domestically located

activities are in several sectors converging on those of foreign investment. Internally, labor market reforms designed to increase flexibility are expected by some to increase total employment. Accompanied by income-insurance programs, the combination of flexible employment with income protection would enhance efficiency while providing material security. Hence, in this scenario, the economic crisis is fading, and in retrospect it will be seen as just a temporary bump on the long-run path of material progress.

The most dire scenario is that there is nothing on the horizon that would reverse the stagnation of low incomes and the insecurity resulting from the disappearance of better-paid jobs. Even if growth does accelerate, there are no grounds to expect that wages would increase at a similar rate. Hence, inequality will continue to increase. Protectionism is unlikely to protect jobs entailing traditional skills, either in industry or in several service sectors. Even if protectionism reduces the outflow of jobs, it will promote labor saving. The very idea of "bringing jobs back" is an empty campaign slogan. While the historical experience has been that replacing people by machines did not reduce total employment much or at all, because new jobs were created in place of those lost, a careful study by the McKinsey Global Institute (2017) concludes that about 60 percent of all occupations currently have at least 30 percent of constituent components that could be automated, and that the rate of increase in employment will slow down. There are also more apocalyptic claims that artificial intelligence is a revolutionary innovation, replacing brains and not just muscles, and that the rate of replacement will be much larger (see Brynjolfsson, Rock, and Syverson 2017). Yet even if the emergence of new jobs compensates for the disappearance of traditional ones, the occupations for which there will be greater demand will be those with low productivity and low wages. The fastest-growing sector in the United States is personal services, the sector with the lowest pay. The US Bureau of Labor Statistics predicts that between 2016 and 2026 non-agricultural wage and salaried jobs will grow at a rate of 0.7 percent per year, with manufacturing jobs declining at an annual rate of 0.6 percent and health care and social assistance jobs increasing at a rate of 1.9 per year. The average annual wage outside agriculture in the United States in 2016 was $49,630, while home health aides earned $23,600 and fast-food cooks $20,570. Among the twenty-eight members of the European Community the fastest-growing sectors between 2008 and 2016 were also the lowest paying ones, with the exception of professional, scientific, and technical workers. Hence, there are reasons to expect that many people will experience the necessity to move to lower-pay occupations, with the attendant loss of social status and a perception of downward mobility.

The distributive effects of this scenario would be alleviated by redistributive income policies. It is intuitive to expect that when inequality increases, so do political demands for redistribution through taxes and transfers or social services: this belief is the cornerstone of political economy. Yet empirical evidence in favor of this theory is at best shaky: indeed, the question "Why don't the poor take it away from the rich?" is a source of unceasing puzzlement, with divergent answers.[1] The,

---

[1] For overviews of this literature, see Putterman (1996), Roemer (1998), Harms and Zink (2003), Lind (2005), Ansell and Samuels (2010), Acemoglu et al. (2015).

not so new, idea on the political horizon in several countries is a universal minimum, "citizen," income. We do need to treat time free from labor not in terms of "unemployment" but as liberation from unnecessary activities, some of which are highly unpleasant. But even if universal income at some decent level is fiscally feasible, it may not be sufficient to overcome ghettoization: the vicious circle of residential segregation, bad schools, unemployment, and crime. Once the ghettoes, "villes," or "barrios" are formed, all policies seem impotent in breaking them. The Right does not know what to do and neither does the Left. Hence, in this scenario, not only inequality but social segregation are here to stay, and perhaps increase.

As we can see, the range of possible economic futures is wide, from the possibility that the crisis would just conveniently disappear to a scenario in which it would become even more profound, without redistribution via the political system. As my description of these possibilities may reveal, I am leaning toward the pessimistic scenario, but perhaps current events in the United States, where the government is embarking on a major program to increase inequality and reduce income protection, unduly colors my more general views. Certainly several European societies are more averse to inequality and several European governments are more attuned to its dangers. I must abdicate to the reader the task of deciding where in this range of possibilities the future lies.

In the political realm, both the left- and the right-wing insurgent parties are "populist." They claim that traditional representative institutions serve the interests of elites and do not provide sufficient voice to "the people." Even though the very word "populism" emerged only at the end of the nineteenth century, such claims are as old as representative institutions. Already, for Anti-Federalists "political aristocracy" was as much of a danger as social aristocracy. If the rulers were other than the ruled, they feared, "Corruption and tyranny would be rampant as they have always been when those who exercised power felt little connection with the people. This would be true, moreover, for elected representatives, as well as for kings and nobles and bishops" (in Ketcham 1986: 18). Hence, they were preoccupied with the duration of terms, as short as six months in New Jersey at one time, term limits, restrictions on representatives to determine their own salaries, and revoking and censuring procedures – almost the same measures as those proposed by President Macron in France.

Representative democracy, the political system ushered in by the American and French revolutions and gradually adopted around the world, recurrently confronts widespread and intense dissatisfaction. Some of this dissatisfaction stems from the intrinsic features of any system in which people decide as a collectivity who will govern them – the limitations of representative democracy that are inevitable yet disagreeable. But some originate from pathologies of the particular systems of representative institutions.

One widespread misunderstanding of the way democracy works is that elections do not offer a choice. The parties offer "tweedledum and tweedledee," "bonnet blanc et blanc bonnet." The Cohn-Bendit brothers (1968) saw elections as a choice between "gin and tonic and tonic and gin," the journalist Friedman (2001) as between "Pepsi or Coke." Clearly, people can choose only between or among the proposals offered by parties; not every conceivable political program is represented in electoral competition. The alternatives that are subject to electoral choice are particularly restricted in systems in which forming new parties is next to impossible, as in the United States, or where the two major parties form grand coalitions. Yet the very fact that individuals are offered little choice on election day does not mean that the people as a collectivity does not choose. What parties propose in elections is what they think is most likely to make them win, and what is most likely to make them win is what most people want. Hence, if parties know exactly what people want, they offer the same platforms and individuals have no choice at the polls; electoral platforms diverge only to the extent that parties are uncertain about individual preferences. Yet had the majority or plurality wanted something different, parties would offer something different; platforms would still converge to the center of public opinion but would be different. Hence, people as a collectivity choose even if individuals have little choice when they cast their votes.

Another source of dissatisfaction is that in elections no single individual decides anything, creating a feeling of inefficacy. When individuals make private choices, they cause outcomes. Yet from an individual point of view, the outcome of an election is independent of one's action. No one can say "I voted for A, therefore A will win"; the most each of us can do is to cast our ballot, go home, and impatiently wait in front of a television set to see how others have voted. When collective decisions are made using a simple majority rule by many individuals endowed with an equal influence over the outcome, no individual has a causal effect on the collective decision. The value of elections is not that each voter has real influence on the final result, but that collective choice is made by summing individual wills. Yet even if people appreciate elections as a mechanism of collective decision making, they still feel politically impotent as individuals.

At the root of the periodic flares of dissatisfaction with representative institutions lies something even more profound. Democracy is a system in which the people decide as a collectivity who will rule them, at least over some period of time. But even if rulers are selected through elections, we are ruled, which means that we are sometimes forbidden to do what some of us would want to do and ordered to do what some of us would not want to do. The ideal that justified the founding of modern representative institutions was "self-government of the people." The problem to be solved, as posed by Rousseau (1964: 182), was to "find a form of association which defends and protects with all the shared force the person and the goods of each associate, and through which each, uniting with all, still obeys but himself, remaining as free as before." But this problem would have a solution only if everyone wanted the same; only then would obeying others be the same as obeying oneself. In a society with conflicting interests and heterogeneous values, being ruled means having to yield to the will of others, against one's own. Democratically elected governments can take money away from some and give it to others, force parents to inoculate their children, keep people in prisons, and in some barbaric countries even kill them. No wonder no one likes being ruled, even if to live together in peace ruled we must be.

These sources of dissatisfaction with representative democracy are just due to the inherent limits imposed on individuals by the requirements of living together in peace. Democracy may still be, and I believe it is (see Przeworski 2010), the least bad way of organizing our lives as a collectivity, but any political arrangements face limits as to what they can achieve. It is only natural that this latent dissatisfaction flares up when democracy does not deliver what people most care about, whether material security, public order, or the realization of cultural values and norms. Hence, there are reasons to expect that postures toward democracy would be outcome-contingent, that democracy may experience crises.

These general features of democracy do not explain, however, the current popularity of "anti-elite," "anti-establishment," "anti-system," populist rhetoric. The slogan of insurgent parties everywhere echoes the cry of Argentine streets during the crisis of 2001: "Everyone Out" ("Fuera Todos"). A cynical interpretation would be that it is just an instrument of outsiders to elbow their way into office by replacing all traditional parties. But is it not true that our representative institutions, as they were designed, favor the interests of elites? There is something inconsistent in bemoaning persistent inequality and at the same time complaining about the populist critique of representative institutions.

Our systems of representative government were born from a fear of participation by the broad masses of the population, a large part of whom were poor and illiterate. One would not err much in thinking that the strategic problem of the "founders," pretty much everywhere, was how to construct representative government for the elites while protecting it from the poor. While governments were to be selected by elections, their role was to ratify the superiority of those entitled to govern by their social and economic position. Created under a shadow of religious and economic conflicts, representative institutions were designed to bar, or at least minimize, the voice of the people between elections, treating all "intermediate organizations" – clubs, associations, trade unions, as well as political parties – as a danger to civil peace. Intended as a bulwark against despotism, they were designed to disable governments from doing much of anything, bad or good, by checking and balancing powers, and by protecting the status quo from the will of the majority. The poor were instructed that their interests would be represented by the wealthy, women that their interests would be guarded by men, the "uncivilized" that they needed to be guided by their colonizers. When the fear for property took hold, self-government, equality, and liberty were dressed up in elaborate intellectual constructions to make them compatible with the rule by a few. The people cannot be trusted because it can "err": James Madison said it, Simón Bolivar said it, and so did Henry Kissinger, when he declared that President Allende was elected "due to the irresponsibility of the Chilean people."

The particular forms of our representative institutions were designed to protect the status quo – whatever it was, but centrally the property relations against temporary majorities. Bicameralism and presidential veto power meant that the status quo could be altered only by super-majorities. Restrictions of franchise, open voting, and indirect elections protected the political influence of elites. These trenches protecting property were gradually removed: suffrage became

universal, ballots secret, elections direct, legislatures more frequently unicameral. Yet they were replaced by new anti-majoritarian mechanisms: judicial review (Ginsburg and Versteeg 2012), delegation of monetary policy to non-elected central banks (Cukierman, Edwards, and Tabellini 1992), and independent regulatory bodies. The 1992 Maastricht Treaty, which restricted annual deficits to no more than 3 percent of GDP, deprived European governments of the possibility to pursue anti-cyclical economic policies and put bounds on social expenditures.

Even without these institutional trenches, elections are inherently an elitist, Manin (1997) would say "aristo-cratic," mechanism. Voters recognize that not everyone is equally equipped to govern, and they elect people whom they see as in some ways distinct. Voters are free to take any qualities they want as signs of this capacity, but most want to vote for people different from themselves. The result is that in no country does the composition of the elected bodies even vaguely resemble the composition of the electorate. The United States Senate is a "millionaires club." Perhaps most ironically the 2017 French legislative elections, won by a party campaigning on anti-elite slogans, generated a parliament even more elitist in terms of education and income than the outgoing one.

When the Italian political philosopher, Norberto Bobbio (1987), analyzed the differences between democracies and dictatorships, all he could come up with was the distinc-tion between systems in which "elites propose themselves and elites impose themselves." But people have no power in a system ruled by elites. No wonder then that calls for institutional reforms that would make "the voice of the people" louder, and some measures toward "direct democracy," dominate the populist institutional agenda. Some of these proposals return to the Anti-Federalist demands mentioned above: short terms, term limits, revocation of mandates, reduction of pay of legislators, and limitations on circulating between the public and private sectors. In the United States, the obvious measures would be direct elections of the president and the delegation of electoral districting from state legislatures to independent bodies. In Europe, such proposals range from the inane, such as the "survey democracy" advocated by the Five Stars (*Cinque Strelle*) party in Italy, to increased reliance on popular initiative referendums, to convocations of randomly selected "paralegislatures" (bodies of randomly selected citizens that consider particular legislative proposals without having the authority to adopt laws). Particularly interesting is a proposal that surged during the last French elections, according to which voters would be able to cast votes for "none of the above" (*vote en blanc*), and if such votes would win a plurality, another election would be called, with none of the previous candidates eligible to present themselves. One wonders what this mechanism would have produced in the US 2016 presidential elections: most likely, neither Trump nor Clinton.

Yet, as justified as the populist dissatisfaction with the extant representative institutions may be, all such measures are no more than palliatives. They may temporarily restore some confidence in democratic institutions, but they hurl themselves against the inescapable: the mere fact that each of us must be ruled by someone else and being ruled must entail policies and laws we do not like. There are gradations – some institutional frameworks induce better representation than others – but in the end, as J.S. Mill (1991) observed, it is not possible for everyone to rule at the same time. Hence, even if some institutional reforms emerge from the current crisis, I fear that they will not change much.

"Europe" is a topic apart. Both the European Union and the Eurozone offer attractive targets for populists. For one, there is no subject, no "the people" in singular, they can possibly represent. Moreover, they are even more distant from the people in plural than their respective governments. The criticism that they are ruled by foreign, often read as "German," elites is plausible. Hence, the calls for isolation and protectionism are appealing.

I am more sanguine about the electoral menace of the radical Right. While several traditional parties are already accommodating the anti-immigration sentiments, electoral victories of the radical Right are not on the horizon in most European countries. The radical Right seems to have a hard core of supporters of about one-fourth of the potential voters in most developed democracies. Trump won only because he was able to take over a traditional party, and many people voted for him because they hated the Clintons, not because of his personality or program. My guess is that the genie is already out of the bottle and that it grew as much as it possibly could.

Yet I doubt that policies directed against "immigration," either by radical Right parties in office or by centrist parties responding to its menace, will appease anyone. While the Right adopts the language of "national sovereignty" and campaigns for measures to control the current flow of people across borders, such measures will have no effect on the ethnic, cultural, and religious conflicts that tear societies apart. The sources of these conflicts are not at the borders; they are deeply embedded in the social fabric. Moreover, polarization has now reached the basic unit of social structure: the family. In 1960, 5 percent of Republican sympathizers and 4 percent of Democratic ones would have been displeased if their offspring were to marry across party lines, while in 2010 these percentages were forty-nine for Republicans and thirty-three for Democrats. Political polarization has deep roots and it will not go away with contingent political events.

While these are just speculations, suppose that nothing much will change in the foreseeable future: growth will be slow, inequality and segregation will persist, good jobs will continue dwindling, and traditional parties will accommodate anti-immigration sentiments while trying to cope with inequality and segregation using the same repertoire of policies. Does such a scenario threaten democracy?

The danger is that democracy would gradually and surreptitiously deteriorate. This is the danger that incumbents may intimidate the hostile media and create a propaganda machine of their own; that they would politicize security agencies, harass political opponents, use state power to reward sympathetic private firms, selectively enforce laws, provoke foreign conflicts to monger fear, and rig elections. The danger in the countries where the radical Right does not accede to office is that governments might go too far in accommodating nativist and racist demands, and restrict civil liberties without

improving the material conditions of the people most dissatisfied with the status quo.

Hence, we should not be desperate but also not sanguine. Something profound is going on. Perhaps the best
diagnosis of the current situation in many democracies is
"intense partisanship with weak parties" (Azari 2016).
Democratic elections peacefully process conflicts only when
political parties are successful in structuring conflicts and
channeling political actions into elections. Representative
institutions absorb conflicts only if everyone has the right to
participate within these institutions, if conflicts are structured
by political parties, if parties have the capacity to control their
supporters, and if these organizations have the incentives to
pursue their interests through the representative system.
My fear is that neither the government of Trump, nor
Brexit, nor the governments that will be elected on the
European continent will improve the everyday lives of most
people, which will only strengthen "anti-establishment" or
"anti-system" sentiments. In a typical election about one in
two voters ends up on the losing side. In presidential systems
the winner rarely receives much more than 50 percent of the
vote, and in parliamentary multi-party systems the largest
share is rarely higher than 40 percent. Moreover, many people
who voted for the winners are dismayed with their performance in office. So most of us are left disappointed, either
with the outcome or with the performance of the winner. Still,
election after election, most of us hope that our favorite
candidate will win the next time around and will not disappoint. It is, thus, only natural that when people participate in
successive elections, see governments change, and discover

that their lives remain the same, they find something wrong with "the system" or "the establishment."

As a Polish adage has it, "A pessimist is but an informed optimist." I am moderately pessimistic about the future. I do not think that the very survival of democracy is at stake in most countries, but I do not see what would get us out of the current discontent. It will not be alleviated by contingent political events, the results of future elections. This crisis is not just political; it has deep roots in the economy and in society. This is what I find ominous.

Acemoglu, Daron, and James Robinson. 2000. "Why Did the West Extend the Franchise? Democracy, Inequality, and Growth in Historical Perspective." *Quarterly Journal of Economics* 115: 1167–99.

Acemoglu, Daron, Suresh Naidu, Pascual Restrepo, and James A. Robinson. 2015. "Democracy, Redistribution, and Inequality." *Handbook of Income Distribution*, Vol. 2. Amsterdam: Elsevier. Pages 1886–966.

Acemoglu, Daron, David Autor, David Dorn, Gordon H. Hanson, and Brendan Price. 2016. "Import Competition and the Great United States Employment Sag of the 2000s."*Journal of Labor Economics* 34(S1): S141–S198.

Acherbach, Joel, and Scott Clement. 2016. "America Really is More Divided Than Ever." *Washington Post*, July 16.

Ageron, Charles-Robert. 1976. "L'opinion française devant la guerre d'Algérie." *Revue française d'outre mer* 231: 256–85.

Akerlof, George A. 1991. "Procrastination and obedience." *American Economic Review* 81: 1–19.

Albright, Jeremy. 2010. "The Multidimensional Nature of Party Competition." *Party Politics* 16: 699–719.

Alon, Amos. 2002. *The Pity of It All: Portrait of the German-Jewish Epoch 1743–1933*. New York: Picador.

Altamirano, Carlos. 1979. *Chili: les raisons d'une défaite*. Paris: Flammarion.

Alvarez, Michael, José Antonio Cheibub, Fernando Limongi, and Adam Przeworski. 1996. "Classifying Political Regimes." *(ACLP) Studies in International Political Development* 31: 3–36.

Andrews, Rhys, Sebastian Jilke, and Steven Van de Walle. 2014. "Economic Strain and Perceptions of Social Cohesion in Europe: Does Institutional Trust Matter?"*European Journal of Political Research* 53: 559–79.

Ansell, Christopher, and David Samuels. 2010. "Democracy and Redistribution, 1880–1930: Reassessing the Evidence." Paper presented at the Annual Meeting of the American Political Science Association, Washington, DC.

Armingeon, Klaus, and Kai Guthmann. 2014. "Democracy in Crisis? The Declining Support for National Democracy in European Countries, 2007–2011." *European Journal of Political Research* 53: 424–42.

Armingeon, Klaus, Christian Isler, Laura Knopfel, David Weisstanner, and Sarah Engler. 2016 Comparative Political Data Set. 1960–2014. www.cpds-data.org.

Arzheimer, Kai. 2013. "Working Class Parties 2.0? Competition between Centre Left and Extreme Right Parties." In Jens Rydren (ed.), *Class Politics and the Radical Right*. London, New York: Routledge. Pages 75–90.

Atkinson, Anthony B.,Thomas Piketty, and Emmanuel Saez. 2011. "Top Incomes in the Long Run of History." *Journal of Economic Literature* 49: 3–71.

Austen-Smith, David. 1992. "Strategic Models of Talk in Political Decision Making." *International Political Science Review* 13: 45–58.

Autor, David, David Dorn, and Gordon H. Hanson. 2013. "The China Syndrome: Local Labor Market Effects of Import Competition in the United States." *American Economic Review* 103: 2121–68.

Autor, David, David Dorn, Gordon H. Hanson, and Kaveh Majlesi. 2017. "A Note on the Effect of Rising Trade Exposure on the 2016 Presidential Election." Appendix to Autor et al. "Importing Political Polarization? The Electoral Consequences of Rising Trade Exposure." Working paper.

Ayta, Selim Erdem, Eli Rau, and Susan Stokes. 2017. "Unemployment and Turnout." Working paper, Department of Politics, Yale University.

Azari, Julia. 2016. "Weak Parties with Strong Partisanship Are a Bad Combination." www.vox.com, November 3.

Banks, Arthur S. 1996. Cross-National Time-Series Data Archive. Databanks International.

Bermeo, Nancy. 2016. "On Democratic Backsliding." *Journal of Democracy* 27(1): 5–19.

Bitar, Sergio, and Crisostomo Pizarro. No date. *La Caida de Allende y la Huelga de el Teniente.* Santiago: Las Ediciones del Ornitorrinco.

Bobbio, Norberto. 1987. *Democracy and Dictatorship.* Minneapolis: University of Minnesota Press.

Boix, Carles, Michael Miller, and Sebastian Rosato. 2012. "A Complete Data Set of Political Regimes, 1800–2007." *Comparative Political Studies* 46: 1523–54.

Bon, Frederic. 1978. *Les élections en France.* Paris: Seuil.

Bracher, Karl Dietrich. 1966. "The Technique of the National Socialist Seizure of Power." In Fritz Stern (ed.), *The Path to Dictatorship 1918–1933: Ten Essays by German Scholars.* Garden City, NY: Anchor Books. Pages 113–32.

Brady, David, John Ferejohn, and Aldo Paparo. 2017. "Immigration and Politics: A Seven Nation Study." Working paper.

Bright Line Watch. 2018. "Wave 5." April. http://brightlinewatch.org/wave5/.

Bruno, Michael, and Jeffrey Sachs. 1985. *Economics of Worldwide Stagflation.* Cambridge, MA: Harvard University Press.

Brynjolfsson, Erik, Daniel Rock, and Chad Syverson. 2017. "Artificial Intelligence and the Modern Productivity Paradox: A Clash of Expectations and Statistics." Working paper.

Buchanan, James M., and Gordon Tullock. 1962. *The Calculus of Consent: Logical Foundations of Constitutional Democracy*. Ann Arbor: University of Michigan Press.

Calvert, Randall. 1994. "Rational Actors, Equilibrium, and Social Institutions." In J. Knight and I. Sened (eds.), *Explaining Social Institutions*. Ann Arbor: University of Michigan Press.

Canovan, Margaret. 2002 "Taking Politics to the People: Populism as the Ideology of Democracy." In Yves Meny and Yves Surel (eds.), *Democracies and the Populist Challenge*. New York: Palgrave. Pages 25–44.

Capoccia, Giovanni. 2005. *Defending Democracy: Reactions of Extremism in Interwar Europe*. Baltimore: Johns Hopkins University Press.

Carr, William. 1969. *The History of Germany 1815–1945*. New York: St. Martin's Press.

Case, Anne, and Angus Deaton. 2017. "Mortality and Morbidity in the 21st Century." *Brookings Papers on Economic Activity*. BPEA Conference Drafts, March 23–4.

Cassese, Sabino. 2011. *Lo Stato fascista*. Milano: il Mulino.

Cautres, Bruno. 2018. "Le clivage gauche-droite dans les démocraties modernes." *Cahiers français* 404 (May–June): 52–61.

Cheibub, Jose Antonio. 2007. *Presidentialism, Parliamentarism, and Democracy*. New York: Cambridge University Press.

Cheibub, Jose Antonio, Jennifer Gandhi, and James Raymond Vreeland. 2010. "Democracy and Dictatorship Revisited." *Public Choice* 143: 67–101.

Chen, M. Keith, and Ryne Rohla. 2018. "The Effect of Partisanship and Political Advertising on Close Family Ties." *Science* 360 (June 1): 1020–4.

Chetty, Raj, David Grusky, Maximilian Hell, Nathaniel Hendren, Robert Manduca, and Jimmy Narang. 2016. "The Fading American Dream: Trends in Absolute Income Mobility Since 1940." Working Paper 22910. www.nber.org/papers/w22910.

Chiaramonte, Alessandro, and Vincenzo Emanuele. 2017. "Party System Volatility, Regeneration and De-institutionalization in Western Europe (1945–2015)." *Party Politics* 23: 376–88.

Cohn-Bendit, Daniel, and Gabriel Cohn-Bendit, 1968. *Obsolete Communism: The Left-Wing Alternative.* New York: McGraw-Hill.

Colantone, Italo, and Piero Stanig. 2017. "The Trade Origins of Economic Nationalism: Import Competition and Voting Behavior in Western Europe." *Balfi Carefin Centre Research Paper No. 2017-49.* Università Commerciale Luigi Bocconi, Milan.

Cornell, Agnes, Jørgen Møller, and Svend-Erik Skaaning. 2017. "The Real Lessons of the Interwar Years." *Journal of Democracy* 28: 14–28.

Corvalan, Luis L. 2003. *El Gobierno de Salvador Allende.* Santiago: LOM Ediciones.

Coser, Lewis A. 1964. *The Functions of Social Conflict: An Examination of the Concept of Social Conflict and Its Use in Empirical Sociological Research.* New York: Free Press.

Cukierman, Alex, Sebastian Edwards, and Guido Tabellini. 1992. "Seigniorage and Political Instability." *American Economic Review* 82: 537–55.

Dahl, Robert A. 1971. *Polyarchy: Participation and Opposition.* New Haven: Yale University Press.

Dancygier, Rafaela M. 2010. *Immigration and Conflict in Europe.* New York: Cambridge University Press.

Dancygier, Rafaela M. 2017. *Dilemmas of Inclusion: Muslims in European Politics.* Princeton: Princeton University Press.

Dancygier, Rafaela M., and David D. Laitin. 2014. "Immigration into Europe: Economic Discrimination, Violence, and Public Policy." *Annual Review of Political Science* 17: 43–64.

Delmer, Sefton. 1972. *Weimar Germany: Democracy on Trial.* London: Macdonald.

Denquin, Jean-Marie. 1988. *1958: La Genèse de la Ve République.* Paris: Presses Universtaires de France.

De Vylder, Stefan. 1974. *Allende's Chile: The Political Economy of the Rise and Fall of the Unidad Popular.* Cambridge: Cambridge University Press.

Diamond, Larry. 2002. "Thinking about Hybrid Regimes." *Journal of Democracy* 13(2): 21–35.

Dimsdale, Nicholas, Nicholas Horsewood, and Allard Van Riel. 2004. "Uncmployment and Real Wages in Weimar Germany." University of Oxford Discussion Papers in Economic and Social History, Number 56.

Dixit, Avinash, Gene M. Grossman, and Faruk Gul. 2000. "The Dynamics of Political Compromise." *Journal of Political Economy* 108: 531–68.

Downs, Anthony. 1957. *An Economic Theory of Democracy.* New York: Harper and Row.

Droz, Bernard, and Evelyne Lever. 1991. *Histoire de la Guerre d'Algérie.* Paris: Éditions du Seuil.

Dunn, John. 2000. *The Cunning of Unreason.* Cambridge: Cambridge University Press.

Dunn, Susan. 2004. *Jefferson's Second Revolution: the Election Crisis of 1800 and the Triumph of Republicanism.* Boston: Houghton Mifflin.

Elias, Anwen, Edina Szocsik, and Christina Isabel Zuber. 2015. "Position, Selective Emphasis and Framing: How Parties Deal with a Second Dimension in Competition." *Party Politics* 21: 839–50.

Elster, Jon. 1998. "Deliberation and Constitution Making." In Jon Elster (ed.), *Deliberative Democracy*. Cambridge: Cambridge University Press. Pages 97–122.

Ermakoff, Ivan. 2008. *Ruling Onself Out: A Theory of Collective Abdications*. Durham, NC: Duke University Press.

Esteban, Joan-Maria, and Debraj Ray. 1994. "On the Measurement of Polarization." *Econometrica* 62: 819–51.

Evans, Richard J. 2003. *The Coming of the Third Reich*. Penguin Publishing Group. Kindle Edition.

Fearon, James. 2011. "Self-enforcing Democracy." *Quarterly Journal of Economics* 126: 1661–708.

Ferejohn, John, and Pasquale Pasquino. 2003. "Rule of Democracy and Rule of Law." In Jose Maria Maravall and Adam Przeworski (eds.), *Democracy and the Rule of Law*. New York: Cambridge University Press. Pages 242–60.

Flechtheim, Ossip K. 1966. "The Role of the Communist Party." In Fritz Stern (ed.), *The Path to Dictatorship 1918–1933: Ten Essays by German Scholars*. Garden City, NY: Anchor Books. Pages 89–112.

Foa, Roberto Stefan, and Yascha Mounk. 2016. "The Democratic Disconnect." *Journal of Democracy* 27(6): 5–17.

Fossati, Diego. 2014. "Economic Vulnerability and Economic Voting in 14 OECD Countries." *European Journal of Political Research* 53: 116–35.

Foucault, Martial. 2018. "Les transformations de la sociologie du vote." *Cahiers français* 404 (May–June): 42–51.

Franceinfo. 2017. "En 2016, les actes racistes, antisémites et antimusulmans ont baissé en France, mais pas les actes antichrétiens." February 2. www.francetvinfo.fr/societe/religion/en-2016-les-actes-racistes-antisemites-et-antimusulmans-ont-baisse-en-france-mais-pas-les-actes-antichretiens_2044983.html.

Friedmann, T. 2001. *The Lexus and the Olive Tree: Understanding Globalization*. New York: Anchor Books.

Gargarella, Roberto. 2003. "The Majoritarian Reading of the Rule of Law." In Jose Maria Maravall and Adam Przeworski (eds.), *Democracy and the Rule of Law*. New York: Cambridge University Press. Pages 147–67.

Ginsburg, Tom, and Mila Versteeg. 2012. "The Global Spread of Constitutional Review: An Empirical Analysis." Working paper, University of Chicago Law School.

Ginsburg, Tom, and Aziz Z. Huq. 2018a. "How to Lose a Constitutional Democracy." *UCLA Law Review* 65(1): 78–169.

Ginsburg, Tom and Aziz Z. Huq. 2018b. *How to Save a Constitutional Democracy*. Chicago: University of Chicago Press.

Golder, Matt. 2016. "Far Right Parties in Europe." *Annual Review of Political Science* 19: 477–97.

Goldsmith, Jack. 2018. "Paradoxes of the Deep State." In Cass R. Sunstein (ed.), *Can It Happen Here?* New York: HarperCollins. Pages 105–34.

Graham, Benjamin A.T., Michael K. Miller, and Kaare Strøm. 2017. "Safeguarding Democracy: Powersharing and Democratic Survival." *American Political Science Review* 111: 686–704.

Graf, Rudiger, and Konrad H. Jarausch. 2017. "'Crisis' in Contemporary History and Historiography." www.docupedia.de/zg/Graf_jarausch_crisis_en_2017.

Graham, Matthew, and Milan W. Svolik. 2018. "Democracy in America? Partisanship, Polarization, and the Robustness of Support for Democracy in the United States." Unpublished manuscript, Yale University.

Gramsci, Antonio. 1971 (c.1930). *Prison Notebooks*. New York: International Publishers.

Guiso, Luigi, Helios Herrera, Massimo Morelli, and Tommaso Sonno. 2017. "Demand and Supply of Populism." Discussion Paper 11871. Center for Economic Policy Research, London.

Habermas, Jurgen. 1973. *Legitimation Crisis*. Boston: Beacon Press.

Haffner, Sebastian. 2002. *Histoire d'un Allemand*. Paris: Babel.

Hainmueller, Jens, and Daniel J. Hopkins. 2014. "Public Attitudes Toward Immigration." *Annual Review of Political Science* 17: 225–49.

Harms, Philipp, and Stefan Zink. 2003. "Limits to Redistribution in a Democracy: A Survey." *European Journal of Political Economy* 19: 651–68.

Hastings, Michel. 2018. "Le clivage gauche-droite: disparition ou renouvellement?" *Cahiers français* 404 (May–June): 34–41.

Helpman, Elhanan. 2016. "Globalization and Wage Inequality." Working paper, Department of Economics, Harvard University.

Hofstadter, Richard. 1969. *The Idea of a Party System: The Rise of Legitimate Opposition in the United States, 1780–1840*. Berkeley: University of California Press.

Huber, John, and Ronald Inglehart. 1995. "Expert Interpretations of Party Space and Party Locations in 42 Societies." *Party Politics* 1: 73–111.

Human Rights Brief. 2017. "Xenophobic and Racist Hate Crimes Surge in the European Union." February 28. http://hrbrief.org/2017/02/xenophobic-racist-hate-crimes-surge-eur opean-union/.

Hutchison, Elizabeth Quay, Thomas Miller Klubock, and Nara B. Milanich (eds.). 2013. "The Chilean Road to Socialism: Reform and Revolution." *Chile Reader: History, Culture, Politics*. Durham, NC: Duke University Press. Pages 343–428.

Ignazi, Piero. 1992. "The Silent Counter-Revolution: Hypotheses on the Emergence of Extreme Right-Wing Parties in Europe." *European Journal of Political Research* 22: 3–34.

Ignazi, Piero. 2003. *Extreme Right Parties in Western Europe*. Oxford: Oxford University Press.

Inglehart Ronald F., and Flanagan S.C. 1987. "Value Change in Industrial Societies." *American Political Science Review* 81: 1289–319.

Inglehart, Ronald F., and Pippa Norris. 2016. "Trump, Brexit, and the Rise of Populism: Economic Have-Nots and Cultural Backlash." Faculty Research Working Paper Series, Harvard Kennedy School.

Ivarsflaten, Elisabeth. 2008. "What Unites Right-Wing Populists in Western Europe? Re-examining Grievance Mobilization Models in Seven Successful Cases." *Comparative Political Studies* 41: 3–23.

Jung, Florian. 2011. "Income Inequality, Economic Development, and Political Institutions." Doctoral dissertation no. 3196 presented at the University of St. Gallen.

Kalecki, Michal. 1972 [1932]. "Czy mozliwe jest 'kapitalistyczne' wyjście z kryzysu?" In *Kapitalizm, koniunktura i zatrudnienie*. Warsaw: Państwowe Wydawnictwo Ekonomiczne. Pages 75–81.

Kantar Public. 2018. "Ocena dzialalnosci rzadu, premiera i prezydenta." Online K002/18, January.

Karl, Terry Lynn. 1995. "The Hybrid Regimes of Central America."*Journal of Democracy* 6(3): 72–87.

Kates, Sean, and Joshua Tucker. 2017. "We Never Change, Do We? Economic Anxiety and the Far Right in a Post Crisis Europe." Working paper, Department of Politics, New York University.

Ketcham, Ralph (ed.). 1986. *The Anti-Federalist Papers and the Constitutional Convention Debates*. New York: Mentor Books.

King, Gary, and Langche Zheng. 2007. "When Can History Be Our Guide? The Pitfalls of Counterfactual Inference." *International Studies Quarterly* 51: 183–210.

King, Gary, Ori Rosen, Martin Tanner, and Alexander F. Wagner. 2008. "Ordinary Economic Voting Behavior in the Extraordinary Election of Adolf Hitler." *Journal of Economic History* 68: 951–96.

216

Kitschelt, Herbert. 1994. *The Transformation of European Social Democracy*. Cambridge: Cambridge University Press.

Kriesi, Hanspeter, Edgar Grande, Martin Dolezal, Simon Bornschier, and Timotheos Frey. 2006. "Globalization and the Transformation of the National Political Space: Six European Countries Compared." *European Journal of Political Research* 45: 921–56.

Kriesi, Hanspeter et al. 2012. *Political Conflict in Western Europe*. Cambridge: Cambridge University Press.

Lambrecht Plaza, Karen. 2011. "La Distribución del Ingreso en Chile: 1960–2000." Facultad de Economia y Negocios, Universidad de Chile, Santiago.

Landau, David. 2013. "Abusive Constitutionalism." *University of California at Davis Law Review* 47: 189–260.

Landsberger, Henry A., and Tim McDaniel. 1976. "Hypermobilization in Chile, 1970–1973." *World Politics* 28: 502–41.

Lee, Woojin, and John E. Roemer. 2006. "Race and Redistribution in the United States: A Solution to the Problem of American Exceptionalism." *Journal of Public Economics* 90: 1027–52.

Le Gac Julie, Anne-Laure Olivier, and Raphael Spina. 2015. *La France en chiffres, de 1870 à nos jours: Sous la direction d'Olivier Wieviorka*. Paris: Perrin.

Lenin, Vladimir I. 1959 [1919]. "Letter to the Workers of Europe and America." In *Against Revisionism*. Moscow: Foreign Languages Publishing House. Pages 479–86.

Lepsius, Rainer M. 1978. "From Fragmented Party Democracy to Government by Emergency Decree and Nationalist Socialist Takeover: Germany." In Juan J. Linz and Alfred Stepan (eds.), *The Breakdown of Democratic Regimes: Europe*. Baltimore: Johns Hopkins University Press. Pages 34–79.

REFERENCES

Levitsky, Steve, and Lucan A. Way. 2010. *Competitive Authoritarianism: Hybrid Regimes after the Cold War.* New York: Cambridge University Press.

Lewandowsky, Stephan, Ullrich K.H. Ecker, and John Cook. 2017. "Beyond Misinformation: Understanding and Coping with the 'Post-Truth' Era." *Journal of Applied Research in Memory and Cognition* 6: 353–69.

Lind, Jo T. 2005. "Why Is there So Little Redistribution?" *Nordic Journal of Political Economy* 31: 111–25.

Lindvall, Johannes. 2014. "The Electoral Consequences of Two Great Crises." *European Journal of Political Research* 53: 747–65.

Linz, Juan J. 1978. *The Breakdown of Democratic Regimes: Crisis, Breakdown, and Reequilibration.* Baltimore: Johns Hopkins University Press.

Lippmann, Walter. 1956. *The Public Philosophy.* New York: Mentor Books.

Lipset, Seymour Martin. 1960. *Political Man.* Garden City, NY: Doubleday.

Los mil dias de Allende. 1997. www.cepchile.cl.

Luo, Zhaotian, and Adam Przeworski. 2018. "Subversion by Stealth: Dynamics of Democratic Backsliding." Working paper, Department of Politics, New York University.

Lust, Ellen, and David Waldner. 2015. "Unwelcome Change: Understanding, Evaluating and Extending Theories of Democratic Backsliding." USAID. pdf.usaid.gov/pdf_docs/PBAAD635.pdf.

McCarty, Nolan, Keith Poole, and Howard Rosenthal. 2016. *Polarized America: The Dance of Ideology and Unequal Riches.* Cambridge, MA: MIT Press.

McGann, Anthony. 2006. *The Logic of Democracy: Reconciling Equality, Deliberation, and Minority Protection.* Ann Arbor: University of Michigan Press.

McKinsey Global Institute. 2017. "A Future That Works: Automation, Employment, and Productivity."

Macaulay, Thomas B. 1900. *Complete Writings*, Vol. 17. Boston and New York: Houghton-Mifflin.

Maddison, Agnus. 2011. Statistics on World Population, GDP and Per Capita GDP, 1–2008 AD. www.ggdc.net/maddison/oriindex.htm.

Maeda, Ko. 2010. "Two Modes of Democratic Breakdown: A Competing Risks Analysis of Democratic Durability."*Journal of Politics* 72(4): 1129–43.

Magaloni, Beatriz. 2017. "Thought Piece on How Democracies Fail." Paper presented at the How Do Democracies Fall Apart (And Could it Happen Here)? conference, Yale University, October 6.

Manin, Bernard. 1997. *The Principles of Representative Government.* Cambridge: Cambridge University Press.

Manin, Bernard. 2017. "Les habits neufs de la représentation." *Esprit* 437: 71–85.

Maravall, Jose Maria. 2016. *Demands on Democracy.* Oxford: Oxford University Press.

Maravall, Jose Maria, and Adam Przeworski. 2001. "Political Reactions to the Economy: The Spanish Experience." In Susan C. Stokes (ed.), *Public Support for Economic Reforms in New Democracies.* New York: Cambridge University Press.

Margalit, Yotam M. 2013. "Explaining Social Policy Preferences: Evidence from the Great Recession." *The American Political Science Review* 107: 80–103.

Marks G, L. Hooghe, M. Nelson, et al. 2006. "Party Competition and European Integration in the East and West: Different Structure, Same Causality." *Comparative Political Studies* 39: 158–9.

Martner, Gonzalo. 1988. *El gobierno del presidente Salvador Allende 1970–1973.* Santiago: Editorial LAR.

Marx, Karl. 1934 [1852]. *The Eighteenth Brumaire of Louis Bonaparte.* Moscow: Progress Publishers.

Marx, Karl. 1952 [1851]. *Class Struggles in France, 1848 to 1850.* Moscow: Progress Publishers.

Marx, Karl. 1971. *Writings on the Paris Commune.* Edited by H. Draper. New York: International Publishers.

Marx, Karl. 1979 [1859]. *A Contribution to the Critique of Political Economy.* New York: International Publishers.

Medina, Lucia. 2015. "Partisan Supply and Voters' Positioning on the Left–Right Scale in Europe." *Party Politics* 21: 775–90.

Meeuwis, Maarten, Jonathan A. Parker, Antoinette Schoar, and Duncan I. Simester. 2018. "Belief Disagreement and Portfolio Choice." NBER Working Paper 25108. www.nber.org/papers/w25108.

Miao, Ouyang. 2016. "The Pro-Competitive Effect of Chinese Imports: Amplification through the Input–Output Network." Job Market Paper, Department of Economics, Brandeis University.

Michaels, Walter Benn. 2007. *The Trouble with Diversity: How We Learned to Love Identity and Ignore Inequality.* New York: Henry Holt and Co.

Miliband, Ralph. 1975. *Parliamentary Socialism: A Study in the Politics of Labour.* 2nd edn. London: Merlin Press.

Mill, John Stuart. 1977 [1859]. *The Collected Works of John Stuart Mill, Volume XVIII – Essays on Politics and Society Part I,* edited by J.M. Robson. Toronto: University of Toronto Press.

Mill, John Stuart. 1991 [1857]. *Considerations on Representative Government.* Cambridge: Cambridge University Press.

Minkenberg, Michael. 2000. "The Renewal of the Radical Right: Between Modernity and Anti-modernity." *Government and Opposition* 35: 170–88.

Minow, Martha. 2018. "Could Mass Detentions Without Process Happen Here?" In Cass R. Sunstein (ed.), *Can It Happen Here?* New York: HarperCollins. Pages 313–28.

Montesquieu. 1995 [1748]. *De l'esprit des lois.* Paris: Gallimard.

Moral, Mert, and Roben E. Best. 2018. "On the Reciprocal Relationship between Party Polarization and Citizen Polarization." Paper presented at the 2018 Annual Meeting of the Midwest Political Science Association, Chicago.

Mudde, Cas. 2004. "The Populist Zeitgeist." *Government and Opposition* 39: 541–63.

Navia, Patricio, and Rodrigo Osorio. 2017. "'Make the Economy Scream'? Economic, Ideological and Social Determinants of Support for Salvador Allende in Chile, 1970–3." *Journal of Latin American Studies* 49: 771–97.

Navia, Patricio, and Rodrigo Osorio. 2018. "Attitudes Toward Democracy and Authoritarianism Before, During and After Military Rule: The Case of Chile, 1972–2013." *Contemporary Politics*: 1–23.

NBC. 2017. "U.S. Hate Crimes Up 20 Percent in 2016, Fueled by Election Campaign: Report." March 14. www.nbcnews.com/news/us-news/u -s-hate-crimes-20-percent-2016- fueled-election-campaign-n733306.

ODEPLAN. 1971. *Plan de la Economia Nacional*. Santiago: Oficina de Planificacion Nacional.

O'Donnell, Guillermo. 1994. "Delegative Democracy." *Journal of Democracy* 5(1): 55–69.

Ostrogorskij, Michael. 1981 [1927]. *Democracy and the Organization of Political Parties*. Piscataway, NJ: Transaction Publishers.

Pasquino, Gianfranco. 2008. "Populism and Democracy." In Daniele M. Albertazzi and Duncan McDonnell (eds.), *Twenty-First Century Populism*. New York: Palgrave Macmillan. Pages 15–29.

Pew Research Center. 2015. "More Mexicans Leaving Than Coming to the U.S." November 19. www.pewhispanic.org/2015/11/19/more-mexicans-leaving-than-coming-to-the-u-s/.

Pew Research Center. 2018. "Public Opinion on Abortion." October 15. www.pewforum.org/fact-sheet/public-opinion-on-abortion/.

Piketty, Thomas. 2018. "Brahmin Left vs Merchant Right: Rising Inequality and the Changing Structure of Political Conflict (Evidence from France, Britain and the US, 1948–2017)." *WID. World Working Paper Series* No. 2018/7.

Pizzorno, Alessandro. 1964. "The Individualistic Mobilization of Europe." *Daedalus* (December): 199–224.

Popper, Karl. 1962. *The Open Society and Its Enemies.* London: Routledge and Kegan Paul.

Prothro, James W., and Patricio E. Chaparro. 1976. "Public Opinion and the Movement of the Chilean Government to the Left, 1952–73." In Arturo Valenzuela and J. Samuel Valenzuela (eds.), *Chile: Politics and Society.* New Brunswick, NJ: Transaction Books. Pages 67–114.

Przeworski, Adam. 1986. *Capitalism and Social Democracy.* New York: Cambridge University Press.

Przeworski, Adam. 2010. *Democracy and the Limits of Self-Government.* New York: Cambridge University Press.

Przeworski, Adam. 2015. "Acquiring the Habit of Changing Governments through Elections." *Comparative Political Studies* 48: 1–29.

Przeworski, Adam, and Fernando Limongi. 1997. "Modernization: Theories and Facts." *World Politics* 49: 155–83.

Przeworski, Adam, Gonzalo Rivero, and Tianyang Xi. 2015. "Elections as a Method of Processing Conflicts." *European Journal of Political Economy* 39: 235–48.

Putterman, Louis. 1996. "Why Have the Rabble not Redistributed the Wealth? On the Stability of Democracy and Unequal Wealth." In John E. Roemer (ed.), *Property Relations, Incentives, and Welfare.* London: McMillan. Pages 359–89.

Rodrik, Dani. 2017. "Populism and the Economics of Globalization." Discussion Paper 12119, Centre for Economic Policy Research, London.

Roemer, John E. 1998. "Why the Poor Do Not Expropriate the Rich: An Old Argument in New Garb." *Journal of Public Economics* 70: 399–424.

Rooduijn, Matthijs, and Tjitske Akkerman. 2017. "Flank Attacks: Populism and Left–Right Radicalism in Western Europe." *Party Politics* 23: 193–204.

Rosanvallon, Pierre. 2004. *Le Modèle Politique Français: La société civile contre le jacobinisme de 1789 à nos jours.* Paris: Seuil.

Rosanvallon, Pierre. 2009. "Réinventer la démocratie." *Le Monde*, April 30.

Rothwell, Jonathan. 2017. "Cutting the Losses: Reassessing the Costs of Import Competition to Workers and Communities." Working paper, Gallup, Inc.

Rothwell, Jonathan, and Pablo Diego-Rosell. 2016. "Explaining Nationalist Political Views: The Case of Donald Trump." Working paper, Gallup. Last revised November 2, 2016.

Rousseau, Jean-Jacques. 1964 [1762]. *Du contrat social.* Edited by Robert Derathe. Paris: Gallimard.

Sadurski, Wojciech. 2018. "How Democracy Dies (in Poland): A Case Study of Anti-Constitutional Populist Backsliding." Legal Studies Research Paper No. 18/01, Sydney Law School.

Saiegh, Sebastian. 2009. "Political Prowess or Lady Luck? Evaluating Chief Executives' Legislative Success Rates." *Journal of Politics* 71: 1342–56.

Sanchez-Cuenca, Ignacio. 2003. "Power, Rules, and Compliance." In Jose Maria Maravall and Adam Przeworski (eds.), *Democracy and the Rule of Law.* New York: Cambridge University Press. Pages 62–93.

Schedler, Andreas. 2006. *Electoral Authoritarianism: The Dynamics of Unfree Competition.* Boulder, CO: Lynn Rienner.

Schorske, Carl E. 1955. *German Social Democracy 1905–1917: The Development of the Great Schism.* New York: Harper & Row.

Schumann, Dirk. 2009. *Political Violence in the Weimar Republic, 1918–1933: Fight for the Streets and the Fear of Civil War.* New York: Berghahn Books.

Schumpeter, Joseph A. 1942. *Capitalism, Socialism, and Democracy.* New York: Harper & Brothers.

Shadmehr, Mehdi, and Dan Berhardt. 2011. "Collective Action with Uncertain Payoffs: Coordination, Public Signals and Punishment Dilemmas." *American Political Science Review* 105: 829–51.

Sheppele, Kim Lane. 2013. "The Rule of Law and the Frankenstate: Why Governance Checklists Do Not Work." *Governance* 26: 559–62.

Skinner, Quentin. 1973. "The Empirical Theorists of Democracy and Their Critics: A Plague on Both Houses." *Political Theory* 1: 287–306.

Smulovitz, Catalina. 2003. "How Can the Rule of Law Rule? Cost Imposition through Decentralized Mechanisms." In Jose Maria Maravall and Adam Przeworski (eds.), *Democracy and the Rule of Law.* New York: Cambridge University Press. Pages 168–87.

Sontheimer, Kurt. 1966. "Anti-Democratic Thought in the Weimar Republic." In Fritz Stern (ed.), *The Path to Dictatorship 1918–1933: Ten Essays by German Scholars.* Garden City, NY: Anchor Books. Pages 32–49.

SPLC. 2016. "Update: 1,094 Bias-Related Incidents in the Month Following the Election." December 16. www.splcenter.org/hate watch/2016/12/16/update-1094-bias-related-incidents-month-fol lowing-election.

Spoon, Jae-Jae, and Heike Kluwer. 2015. "Voter Polarisation and Party Responsiveness: Why Parties Emphasise Divided Issues, But Remain Silent on Unified Issues." *European Journal of Political Research* 54: 343–62.

Stern, Fritz. 1966. "Introduction," In *The Path to Dictatorship 1918–1933: Ten Essays by German Scholars.* Garden City, NY: Anchor Books.

Stokes, Susan C. (ed.). 2001. *Public Support for Economic Reforms in New Democracies*. New York: Cambridge University Press.

Stone, Geoffrey R. 2018. *Perilous Times: Free Speech in Wartime, from the Sedition Act of 1798 to the War on Terrorism*. New York: W.W. Norton.

Strauss, David A. 2018. "Law and the Slow-Motion Emergency." In Cass R. Sunstein (ed.), *Can It Happen Here?* New York: HarperCollins. Pages 365–86.

Svolik, Milan W. 2015. "Which Democracies Will Last? Coups, Incumbent Takeovers, and the Dynamic of Democratic Consolidation." *British Journal of Political Science* 45(4): 715–38.

Svolik, Milan W. 2017. "When Polarization Trumps Civic Virtue: Partisan Conflict and the Subversion of Democracy by Incumbents." Unpublished manuscript, Yale University.

SWIID. 2014. "The Standardized World Income Inequality Data Base." Version 4.0. https://dataverse.harvard.edu/dataset.xhtml?persistentId=hdl:1902.1/11992.

Teinturier, Brice. 2018. "Perceptions de la politique et vote: ce qui a changé." *Cahiers français* 404 (May–June): 62–71.

Tingsten, Herbert. 1973. *The Swedish Social Democrats*. Totowa: Bedminster Press.

Turner, Henry Ashby Jr. 1985. *German Big Business and the Rise of Hitler*. New York: Oxford University Press.

UNU-WIDER. 2014. "World Income Inequality Database (WIID3.0A)." June. www.wider.unu.edu/research/WIID-3a/en_GB/database/

Varol, Ozan O. 2015. "Stealth Authoritarianism." *Iowa Law Review* 100: 1673–742.

Wagner, M. 2012. "Defining and Measuring Niche Parties." *Party Politics* 18: 854–64.

Weakliem, David. 2016a. "Declining Support for Democracy?" December 7. https://justthesocialfacts.blogspot.com/2016/12/decl ining-support-for-democracy.html?m=0.

Weakliem, David. 2016b. "Going Downhill." December 2. https:// justthesocialfacts.blogspot.com/2016/12/going-downhill.html? m=0.

Weingast, Barry R. 1997. "Political Foundations of Democracy and the Rule of Law." *American Political Science Review* 91: 245–63.

Weingast, Barry R. 2015. "Capitalism, Democracy, and Countermajoritarian Institutions." *Supreme Court Economic Review* 23: 255–77.

Wilson, Kenneth A. 2017. Cross-National Time-Series Data Archive.

Yocelevzky, Ricardo A. 2002. *Chile: partidos politicos, democracia y dictadura, 1970–1990*. Mexico: Fondo de Cultura Economica.

Zakaria, Fareed. 1997. "The Rise of Illiberal Democracy." *Foreign Affairs* 76(6): 22–43.